Thou Shalt Not

Note for Librarians: A cataloguing record for this book is available from Library and Archives Canada at www.collectionscanada.ca/amicus/index-e.html
ISBN 1-4251-1226-9

Offices in Canada, USA, Ireland and UK

Book sales for North America and international:
Trafford Publishing, 6E–2333 Government St.,
Victoria, BC V8T 4P4 CANADA
phone 250 383 6864 (toll-free 1 888 232 4444)
fax 250 383 6804; email to orders@trafford.com
Book sales in Europe:
Trafford Publishing (UK) Limited, 9 Park End Street, 2nd Floor
Oxford, UK OX1 1HH UNITED KINGDOM
phone +44 (0)1865 722 113 (local rate 0845 230 9601)
facsimile +44 (0)1865 722 868; info.uk@trafford.com
Order online at:
trafford.com/06-2985

10 9 8 7 6 5 4 3 2

CONFESSION

Overwhelmed by adult behavior and due to lack of any logical answers to her questions, Diana started her investigation with the one person who had control over the people in the small town – their parish priest.

"Forgive me father," she humbly said bowing her head as she knelt her tiny body behind the partition in the gym. Her final trivial misbehavior was that of eating and enjoying stolen candies. "Be lenient father for I did not steal them." She was not impressed with her penance of a rosary and decided to question the priest at her next confession.

One month later she knelt in the gym confessing a carbon copy of her sins. Seconds before the father was about to give her the usual penance of a rosary she interrupted him.

"Father, my parents don't have money to pay for masses, does that mean they will go to hell?" She was referring to his sermon of the previous Sunday on how parishioners had the choice of paying for their own masses before they died.

"If you think this is logical father, then why can't we accumulate prayers and use them when we get the urge to sin, like eating stolen candies?" Without giving him a chance to respond she continued her questionings.

"Father, are you allowed to have a girlfriend?" A loud stern 'NO "pierced her ears. "Then why are people talking about you and the woman who lives on Main Street?

The priest was overwhelmed by her questions as he hastily made the sign of the cross and sent her on her way forgetting to give her a penance.

A broad smile covered her face as she slowly walked passed her school friends. Guilt hovered momentarily so she knelt in the corner of the gym, bowed her head and sited a few prayers convinced it was sufficient.

PREFACE

When Colleen approached me about writing the Preface for her book, I wondered whether I could rise to the occasion. Feeling honored and moved by her request, I voraciously read every word of her book. At times I was tempted to skip a few chapters, as certain passages describe so vividly the difficult context of violent and abusive relationships.

Colleen's book is superb, not because it relates an extraordinary tale or takes us into a world of the fantastic, but rather because it exudes truth and humanity. The work is a hymn to resilience, an ability possessed by certain people—no matter what—to get back up on their feet and become stronger while enduring the worst of life's trials.

Sprinkled with humor, the book reveals the destiny of a young girl who survived thanks to an incredible determination. From one anecdote to another, the reader is a witness to her struggle to become a mother worthy of her children, also to this young woman's attempts, in spite of difficulties, at finding happiness in love, and finally to a mature woman driven by love and the power of forgiveness. The book speaks of the very essence of life: personal growth. It tells of courage and of openness; it exalts the power and richness of love. True to the author's own spirit, it is full of spontaneity, of maturity acquired through struggle, of courage that guarantees the success of one's destiny, and of an inspiring will to get on with life.

My encounter with Colleen has moved me profoundly. I was afforded the privilege of being by her side along the difficult path of accepting the loss of her son. She unveiled her mother's heart to me with trust—a faith I found throughout her work. Hers is an endless faith in the beauty of life, often visible only after arduous struggles. It's the miracle of believing in better days ahead, of following one's dreams to the end, of daring to tell all, of simply putting down one's whole life on blank paper, of making one's life public so that it will heal its author, and in all probability, some of its readers too.

Indeed, this book is superb, and it's with a feeling of gratitude that I humbly offer these words in celebration of this work. Thank you, Colleen, for your trust.

Louise Charbonneau
Psychologist
2006/05/06

Tribute to Colleen Jeans

When Colleen asked me to edit her book, "Thou Shalt Not," I wasn't prepared for the impact that her memoirs would have on me. The chronicle of her struggles to survive abusive relationships, let alone raise six children as a single parent and working mother, often impelled me to put my task on hold and read ahead to find out what would happen next.

The anecdotes in "Thou Shalt Not" are conveyed through the eyes of a woman who has experienced the equivalent of several lifetimes rolled into one. As Colleen guides us through an oppressive childhood and into a turbulent adulthood that engulfs her with tragedy and despair, we can't help but have the deepest respect for one who endures so much emotional and physical suffering, yet emerges as a loving person, full of joie de vivre.

Narrated with compassion and a dash of humor, Colleen's exceptional story is candid and sensitive, and tugs at one's heartstrings. Confronted with desperate situations that only a fearless determination can overcome and with deep pain that only the power of forgiveness can heal, Colleen succeeds in putting the past behind her and pursuing her dreams for a happy tomorrow. Her journey is an inspiration to readers and, without doubt, a comfort to those who have walked along a similar path in their lives.

I feel privileged to have met Colleen and to have worked on "Thou Shalt Not" with her. Thank you, Colleen, for including me in your journey.

Sincerely,

Sandra Nikolai
Editor/Writer

This book is dedicated, first of all, to my children, who like little soldiers, stood by my side through life's challenges. Their love and affection have been my reason for life. I have been blessed to be their mom and realize that I had been living with angels.

To my husband, who patiently stood by my side throughout the years as I cleansed my closet of hidden pain.

To my grandchildren who's hugs are like precious jewels for they have given me another reason to love life and live it to the fullest.

To Louise Charbonneau, Psychologist, whose professionalism helped me, rid myself of my inner pain. To Sandra Nikolai, Editor/ Writer, who believed in my story.

And finally, to the very special persons who have crossed my path leaving their heart prints engraved in mine forever.

Although the incidents in *Thou Shalt Not* are true, all the names have been changed.

No incident depicted within is implied in any way to intimidate or otherwise relate to any specific person.

Chapter 1
Forgive Me, Father

A beautiful, crisp, clear winter night greeted us as we threw our marbles onto the icy pond. Simone and I ran and fetched them with carefree abandon, a rush of adrenalin surging through us when we realized we had ventured out a bit too far. Excitement raced through our young minds given that we had challenged the "thou-shalt-not-go-on-the-pond" rule. The risk of danger made it even more exhilarating.

The only light came from a sky filled with a million stars. Majestic fir trees stood in all their glory, branches bowed with layers of snow. The air was still, and the silence gave everything a fairy tale quality. Even though it was cold and dark, our hearts overflowed with fun and laughter, void of fear or remorse.

The sound of howling and barking in the distance gave us a feeling of security. I hadn't realized the danger ahead until I threw a marble a little too far, ran too fast, fell, and slid like hot butter across the ice and into the freezing water. The weight of my wool trousers was dragging me down, and a vise-like pressure forced the last bit of air out of my lungs. Everything began to move in slow motion.

All of a sudden, a pulling sensation yanked me toward the opening in the ice. Had I unconsciously found my way up? I gasped for air as I surfaced and frantically clutched onto the ice, but a piece broke away, then another, until I finally managed to grab hold of a solid chunk and heaved myself out. I looked around. I was alone. Surely Simone had gone to get help.

My body grew numb. The stars seemed so close that I felt as if I were floating among them. With the sudden realization that I might die alone, an uncontrollable fear swept over me. I began to pray. Never had I prayed the "Our Father" with such intensity and sincerity. I knew I had disobeyed. I was surely on my way to hell. I feared the consequences. Most of all, I feared God. Filled with remorse, I promised to never disobey Him again.

I noticed shadows in the distance walking toward me. The last thing I remembered was seeing a blur of faces and hearing conversation that didn't make any sense before I drifted into unconsciousness.

I awoke bundled in a wool blanket in front of the wood stove. Dad was forcing hot red wine down my throat. I passed out—either from too much wine or a dipping body temperature. Whatever the reason, I regained consciousness three days later.

Where was I? Who were these people around me? Why was everyone so excited? I recognized the doctor, the priest, of course, and Mom and Dad. I felt it was inappropriate to let my eyes meet with the priest's. I was certain he knew I had disobeyed. Disobedience was a sin, and if a priest visited a house, it was bad news. Only fever or the consequences of sin could bring an innocent mind to places it dreads.

The priest wore a long black robe, and his pale face was masked with righteousness as he stood next to the bed and stared down at me. He had administered the last sacrament. I knew what that meant: I had teetered on the threshold of death. His beady eyes danced with delight and his lips curled up in gratification for having saved yet another soul. I had pneumonia, but I had survived. Thank you, God. I will never disobey or sin again. I promise.

God knows that promises made through fear, especially from a child, will undoubtedly be broken. But as I made these promises, I was engulfed in intense contrition. I was certain that I was having a one-on-one conversation with God and that He had forgiven me.

A few days later, Mom and Dad went shopping in the nearest town—eighteen miles away. It was thirty degrees below zero.

Beneath the house was a crawl space used for storing food. Since we were unaware of the severity of my illness, Timmy, my younger brother, and I snuck down the ladder and closed the trap door behind us. We dug a hole in the sandy wall and placed a flashlight in it. We lay flat on our stomachs and laughed hysterically as we drove our wooden cars across the frozen earth. I didn't feel the damp, bone-chilling air and went on playing for hours.

All at once, I realized how small the crawl space was. A sudden fear along with a tightening sensation in my chest overpowered me. I panicked and began to hyperventilate, then coughed uncontrollably. "Timmy, we must go up now. Mom and Dad will soon be home. We're not allowed to come down here," I said as I tugged on his sleeve and urged him to hurry.

That night, I developed a high fever and chills, and began to hallucinate. I had had a relapse. After several days, the fever subsided. When I opened my eyes, the first person I saw was my father sitting next to me. "Dad?" I whispered.

He didn't answer. Concern and intense sadness camouflaged the usual mean look in his dark blue eyes. I was surprised when I learned that he had sat with me during the three days I was fighting for my life.

I was ten years old and recovery was quick. Life continued without disrupting the usual activity in the house—violent or otherwise. The mere smell of spring air boosted our youthful energy levels. Before the fields of mud had dried, our agendas were overflowing with plans and mischief.

Chapter 2
Growing Pains

Thou shalt not steal, thou shalt not lie, and thou shalt not. Growing up in the 1940s was hard enough without having to fear that every action or thought that crossed my young mind was on the sin list. I believed in God the Father Almighty, forgiveness of sins, love thy neighbor, charity, honor thy father and thy mother, and so on. Angels of God with pristine crystal little minds, we were born unaware that religion would brand us with the fear of sin and damnation. Parents, teachers, and other adults handed us an endless list of priorities to live by if we wanted to attain the privileged rewards of heaven.

My mind wanders back a generation, to fields filled with weeds and flowers, where clean air played an indispensable role in our survival. I lived in the country, and nature was my playground. The trees were for climbing, the fields were for running, and the forests were for playing hide-and-go-seek. As part of our daily routine, we had rules to follow. We memorized the list of do's and don'ts, but as much as we tried to follow these rules, we were often enticed by nature and its beauty. We ran off to play and forgot about our obligations, only to suffer the consequences of our neglect.

Our family of seven lived in a modest home that measured less than five hundred square feet. Nanette was ten years old and the eldest child in the family, followed by me—Diana, Timmy, Billy, and Sissy. On the first floor were the kitchen, living room, Dad's den, two bedrooms, and a bathroom. A wood stove was used for cooking and heating the home, and supplied us with hot water. A red pump that sat on the kitchen counter provided cold spring water all year round. At the top of the second floor, a tiny hallway served as sleeping space for Sissy. A bedroom bordered either side of the hallway: one for the girls and one for the boys.

Nothing but holy pictures and crucifixes decorated the beige walls. The only one we paid attention to was Mom's statue of St. Jude. If the statue was facing the wall, we knew Mom was upset with her saint because he hadn't responded to her requests.

"Mom, can you ask him to do a favor for me?" I asked.

"Pray to him yourself, Diana; he will help you," she replied.

"That's all right, Mom, I don't know him, and he doesn't know me. I'd be wasting my time. He's your friend."

I didn't want to pray to a silly statue anyway. It was tea time and my sister was calling me to go play with her.

In the field behind the house, Dad had built a beautiful dollhouse for Nanette and me. It had windows with curtains, homemade furniture, and a set of dishes. Since I had always played the role of the Dad, I asked Nanette to exchange roles so that I could be the Mom for one day. After I pleaded with her over and over, she reluctantly agreed.

My sister Nanette was my best friend. But like most relationships between sisters, ours wasn't perfect. It offered moments of sibling rivalry as we went through the growing pains of our youth—and this was one of them. With revenge still fresh on my eight-year-old mind, I wondered what I could do that wouldn't hurt my sister but would make me feel good? Amazingly enough, I found the solution. I urinated in the teapot.

The next day, Nanette and I were sitting at the table in the dollhouse. We were eating lunch and pretending to be adults, but to my surprise, Nanette decided not to have tea that day. I didn't tell my sister what I had done for fear she'd run to Mom or Dad. I avoided a confrontation with Dad but it cost me. The price of my sin was guilt, and I didn't like the penalty.

#

My friend Simone lived in the next house over. Our last major dare was that of the marbles on the icy pond. Simone spoke no friendship gave us the perfect opportunity to learn each other's language. I soon became bilingual and thought I could understand what the quarrels between my parents were all about. They spoke to us in English but quarreled in French. But having learned French gave me no advantage in understanding why my parents argued so much. It still sounded like jargon to me.

Simone's father was a farmer who owned a few cattle. An electric wire fence restrained the livestock on his property from wandering off too far. One day, my father and a few of his friends were building a shed inside the fenced area. Timmy and I were playing tag on the outer side of the fence when one of the men deliberately dropped his hammer and called out for our help.

The fence was too high for us to jump over it, so we tried to crawl underneath it instead. The jolt from the fence stunned us. When Dad and his friends burst out laughing, Timmy and I understood at once how we had succeeded in satisfying their barbaric sense of humor. It seemed as if we couldn't do anything to make Dad like us—not even a little. We tried, but he didn't. He couldn't.

Surprisingly, I do have one earlier memory of having witnessed an act of thoughtfulness on Dad's part. It happened when we were living in a tiny town next to a train track, before we moved to the country. One Easter morning, we awoke to a wonderful surprise. Beautiful French doors stood between the kitchen and the living room, but on this particular morning, they were shut. Sticking out from under the doors were strings with our names attached to them. We gently pulled on the strings, but something prevented us from pulling any further. As Dad slowly opened the doors, a twinkle materialized in his blue eyes, and a look of pride swept over his face. It was one of the happiest expressions I had ever seen.

Behind the doors, hand-made rabbits and ducks painted in beautiful pastel colors pulled little wooden trains on wheels. Candies and homemade cookies filled the wagons. We were the luckiest children in the world that Easter morning, and we couldn't stop thanking Dad. We wanted to hug him, but hugging wasn't encouraged in my family. However, we were allowed a quick hug. We didn't get hugged back, though, as Dad's arms hung limply by his side.

We played with our toys for hours. Our joy cancelled out all previous bad memories. The ability to store bad memories far away in our minds was a gift. All we knew at that moment was that we had the best Dad.

I later understood the effort my father had put into this surprise. He was a carpenter and had taken the time to carve the animals, carts, and wheels by hand, and had painted them—all without our knowledge. That day, I saw pride and love in his eyes.

Later I was playing ball in the streets next to the train tracks. A train was whistling in a distance when I accidentally dropped the ball. It headed straight toward the tracks. I had become so accustomed to the sound of the train that I ran after the ball, not giving it a second thought. I was nearing the tracks when someone pulled me back and threw me onto the gravel road.

I looked up to see Dad trembling as he stood over me. His eyes were dark blue—a deep shade of blue they became whenever he was furious. In spite of having saved me from the oncoming train, he beat the daylights out of me with his black leather strap when we arrived home. I knew I deserved it this time, but it also told me he cared. It was a daisy day. I love you. I love you not.

#

Chores were a large part of growing up in the country. During the summer holidays, laughter filled the air as we chopped wood and piled it into cords, and made sure the icebox never ran out of ice. Weeding the garden and cleaning the stables were a must, as was cleaning the house.

Timmy and I were responsible for carefully piling the wood in the backyard. One day, after we had finished the task, we set off down the trail to play. Soon we noticed billows of smoke rising from behind our home. Six-year-old Billy had set fire to the wood.

I expected Dad to punish Billy since all the wood had burnt to the ground, but Dad didn't even scold him. Mom's "favorite" child had escaped punishment once again.

As if to make up for the beatings he never gave Billy and Nanette, Dad's violent streak intensified toward Timmy and me over time, but his rage wasn't restricted to people. One afternoon, Timmy and I picked up a stray dog a few miles from home and immediately made him a member of our family. We knew Dad didn't like animals, but we never believed he'd hurt them. The dog was timid, and he growled at Billy. When Dad saw this, he grabbed the dog and strangled it in front of us.

I was devastated and felt that it was my fault the dog was dead. I wondered why I had even brought the poor creature home. Timmy was especially heartbroken. He had often wished he could own a dog. But when Dad told us we weren't allowed to take in any other strays because it was a distraction for us and kept us from doing our daily chores, Timmy's hopes were dashed forever.

I was certain that, had the dog had bitten off Timmy's nose, Dad would have interpreted it as an accident and nothing more. At times, I strongly resented Dad's preference for my younger brother Billy and older sister Nanette. They also seemed to escape Dad's wrath more often than Timmy and I ever did. But my anger was easily erased when my siblings offered me a simple smile.

#

Weekends meant house cleaning as Nanette and I diligently washed, scrubbed, and swept the house from top to bottom. Our brothers didn't think twice about walking in with sand on their clothes and in their shoes. They figured it was our job to clean up after everyone.

"I swear, Nanette, I will never have boys when I grow up. Their rooms are always filthy," I complained every week.

But at the end of the day, my sister and I looked around and proudly admired our impeccable work—despite the setbacks.

Payback time arrived on Saturday evenings when we took turns bathing in a square tub that sat in the middle of the kitchen. "Girls first" had a pleasant ring to it as Nanette and I enjoyed the hot clean water before our brothers did. But nothing surpassed our preference for washing our hair outdoors. The sound of thunder behind dark skies especially triggered our excitement, and Nanette and I reached for the bar of homemade soap and raced outside. We laughed and danced like little fairies, around and around in the pouring rain, our heads full of suds. We were oblivious to the spectacular elements of lightening, but our screams and laughter caught Mom's attention, and she peeked outside through the curtains from time to time—probably concerned about what the neighbors might be thinking.

Chapter 3
Generation Gap

My mother was beautiful, tall, and slim, and had dark hair and blue eyes. She was the oldest and the prettiest of her siblings, and the one that accomplished something significant in her life: she was a schoolteacher. As is customary in the village where she was raised, everyone knew everyone else's business. They went to mass on Sundays wearing their fancy hats and outfits, and displaying hypocritical moments of remorse that were normally reserved for the confessional. After mass, they returned home, only to continue with their lives in secrecy. Everyone in the entire neighborhood knew everyone else's dirty little secrets but never let on.

Mom had been dating a prospector friend who was deeply in love with her. One day, a handsome, well-dressed stranger arrived in the quiet little village. He was a small man with piercing blue eyes and a well-trimmed mustache. It didn't take long for the schoolteacher's path to cross his. After they met, the prospector dropped out of the picture, and a new romance began.

The relationship between the schoolteacher and the stranger became the main topic of conversation in town. The couple didn't even take the time to get acquainted before they rushed down the altar to get married. After Mom and Dad had settled down and began to decorate their home, Dad hung a picture of a beautiful woman in their bedroom—that of his late wife who had died shortly after the birth of their first son. The picture stayed on the wall, and Mom never questioned it, which was what she believed an obedient wife should do.

My grandmother had molded Mom to be just like her—a hard-working woman, religious and dutiful to her husband. Our bodies, the priests, and Mom's father were subjects that Mom did not allow us to discuss. Anything that might disrupt the pristine image that Mom thought she projected to those around her was forbidden. Sex was a sin, so curiosity about sex was not allowed. Not even the slightest whisper.

But as generations passed, different hopes and dreams, and dares and audacity silently surfaced, overcoming the process and cycle of wishful cloning. The realization of individuality was in progress—and it began with me.

#

I loved visiting my grandmother. She was a short, stubby lady with white hair and beautiful blue eyes. I hugged her and actually get an honest warm hug back. Every time she wrapped her arms around me, I couldn't get enough of the scent of her inexpensive apple blossom perfume.

The delicious smell of food boiling on the stove and homemade bread in the oven was irresistible, and at times I wished I lived there. I had often wondered how Grandma's apron remained spotless until I saw her wipe her hands on the backside of her dress. I peeked and noticed that it was covered with remnants of her daily cooking.

Whenever my grandfather approached me, the putrid stench of cigar, rotting teeth, and alcohol blocked the culinary aromas from my nasal cavities. I hastily distanced myself from him and tried to regain the pleasant scent of Grandma and her cooking.

Every time I visited Grandma, she weighed me in the hope that I had gained a few pounds, but I never did. She weighed me again before sending me back home. I devoured plenty of food at her place, but even so, I never gained an ounce.

As for my grandfather ... well, I kept my distance from him. He teased me a lot and had a habit of touching me when we played. His left hand had been torn off from dynamite he had used to blow up tree stumps while preparing the fields for gardening. He had also lost his left eye and his hearing, and had a problem with his left leg.

Granddad worked at a liquor store, so he was able to appease his love for "the bottle" whenever he wanted. He often sat in his rocking chair and chewed tobacco. With his one eye, he examined my every move. Whenever I missed the bus home from his house—something that frequently occurred due to his "forgetfulness" to have me arrive at the bus stop in time—he drove the eighteen miles to bring me back home. On the way, he teased me a lot and pretended he was tickling me. He laughed out loud, thinking he could distract me as his hand slowly made its way up my dress. He wanted me to believe it was accidental, but these accidents were happening too often.

A time came when he assumed that I felt safe with him. He stopped the car at the side of the road. Even though he had but one good hand, I felt as if he had many more as he roamed over my five-year-old body like a frenzied shark, using his handless arm as a weapon. I froze, stunned by what he was doing. Because I believed that certain body parts were sinful, my thighs welded together and became one. Every nerve and muscle tightened, making it impossible for him to penetrate.

Granddad's grunting and swearing scared me. I began to whisper the Lord's Prayer. Then it was finally over. Major sin, this I knew for sure, but whose sin was it?

I can still remember Granddad's white-and-blue blurred eye and his toothless mouth slobbering as he cursed God. I gasped for air, but the only air available for me to breathe contained the thick stomach-turning odor of brown rotting teeth and alcohol that filled the car.

Suddenly he let go of me and turned on the ignition. He hadn't expected such a fight. He was furious, and I was hoping he felt humiliated. The emotional extortionist and master thief of self-confidence and destroyer of trust had failed once again.

When we were on the last mile home, he turned toward me. He reassured me that everything was fine and that I was a good little girl, but he warned that I mustn't tell anyone what had happened. "You mustn't tell your Mom. She's frail and she'll be angry with you," he said with a grunt.

I slowly rolled down the window and took a deep breath of air. Then I turned to look at him and said, "Take me home please, Granddad."

"It is best that you keep this a secret; it will be our secret." He let out a nervous laugh.

I didn't speak because I was afraid to say something wrong. Above all, I didn't want to delay the trip home. He stared into my eyes and nodded his head, hoping I'd give him a sign of understanding or reassurance. But he was staring into young eyes filled with hate and fear. He had now made his mark. His name was second on the bad man's list engraved in my mind.

Back home, Granddad's first reaction was to tell Mom that I was a good little girl and that he'd like me to visit him the following weekend. She smiled and kissed him goodbye. As she walked him to the car, I heard her ask what time she should send me.

Mom hadn't closed the front door behind her yet when I burst in tears. "Mom, I don't want to go back to Granddad's," I screamed.

She pointed to the stairs and sent me off to bed.

I refused and tried to explain why I didn't want to go back. "Mom," I said, yelling and crying uncontrollably, "Granddad was touching me. He was hurting me and trying to take my clothes off. He didn't want me to tell you because you're sick or something." I gasped for air with each sentence.

I might as well have confided in my rag doll because Mom had no reaction. Yelling, answering back, even saying no were grounds for punishment, let alone another entry on my sin list. She pointed to the stairs one more time with no indication that she had believed me. I went to bed with a broken heart and cried myself to sleep that night with a rosary in my hands. I prayed I'd never become an adult. Adults were the ones who preached the laws that they continuously broke day after day.

From that day on, my grandfather never gave up. He had one thing in mind, and every moment he spent alone with me, he tried again. But he never succeeded. I was the granddaughter who never wanted to sit on his lap. His attempts, even in public, were in vain. For me, any excuse to stay away from him was valid. My aunts and uncles couldn't understand why I persistently avoided him.

I was a feisty little girl who knew right from wrong, and his intentions were extremely wrong. After my first experience and Mom's reluctance to listen to my pleas, I took matters into my own hands. My grandfather never did get the best of me; no matter how hard he tried. What he didn't know was that, every time he failed, I grew stronger. His frustration with me didn't blur my thinking. I anticipated his intentions and tactics. I became wiser in avoiding situations that might make me vulnerable, although he never gave up trying.

When my grandfather died, I was a teen. I was sad to see my mother cry, and I didn't like the idea of death. But as they slowly lowered my grandfather's coffin into the ground, I grabbed handfuls of earth and threw them at the coffin. Filled with rage, I screamed, "Take it with you, Granddad. Take them all with you, your sins." The more I cried, the angrier I became. "They are not mine; take them with you."

But no one paid attention to me. I supposed they were concentrating on their own loss and weren't alarmed by the ranting of a young girl. As for me, I had wiped the slate clean. I had buried the sin and guilt with him and had forgiven him. He'd have to explain his actions and pay the price when he arrived on the other side. My debilitating anger and the heavy anchors of hatred and rage would have taken too much space in my heart anyway. They would have kept me from learning how to practice the best gift ever—the gift of forgiveness.

Chapter 4
Nocturnal Escapes

The picture of Dad's first wife had hung in my parents' bedroom for more than a decade. I supposed that Mom didn't like the idea of it hanging there, but she never opposed Dad's wish for fear of getting him angry. However, she did wonder what had happened to the baby boy after his mother had died.

"Junior" had been raised by his grandmother and was sent back home to Dad at the age of twelve. It was hinted that Junior's grandmother was attempting to ignite the relationship between Dad and the firstborn son he had abandoned years earlier.

I was four years old when Junior came to live with us, so I have few memories of him, except for one that still haunts me. About a year after Junior had moved in with us, he led me to a huge tree near the house. He was excited as he showed me a heart he had carved into the tree with his initials and that of his little girlfriend.

"I promise not to tell anyone, Junior, cross my heart and spit to die." I spit on the ground to seal my promise.

All of a sudden, Dad grabbed Junior from behind and flung him in the air. Dad had always blamed Junior for his wife's death. Everything his son did was bad and deserved a beating. It was as if Dad had to teach him a lesson.

Later I heard Junior crying in his room. That was the last I heard of him. He ran away from home that same night with stolen cash and cookies—just as Dad had done at the same age—and hitched a ride on a passing train to return to his grandmother's home.

Hats off to you, half brother, you had the courage to leave. I'm so proud of you.

Dad was frustrated when he learned about the stolen money. But Mom's face lit up in delight—her stepson had liked her cookies enough to steal them all. I supposed she hadn't understood that the cookies had formed part of his survival kit.

Junior's departure gave Mom a mission. She wanted to get Dad and his son back together again. She tried hard but without success. My half brother didn't return to our house until Dad died. When he showed up for Dad's funeral, money was the main reason. But Junior suffered disappointment. Dad had cashed in his insurance policy and had drunk every last penny of it. He believed that everyone should work for his money, and he wasn't going to hand down any of it.

I wondered what kind of life Junior had made for himself. Had he accumulated anger, pain, and frustration, and then let it go by sharing it with his family? Or had he allowed the hurt to swell inside until it disrupted his health and the lives of the ones he loved?

Lucky for Junior that he hadn't met up with Dad the night he decided to run away. Dad's rages were usually nocturnal. In the deep silence of the night, when dreams were floating in our young minds, he crept up the stairs, carrying an overload of suppressed anger that he released on one of us.

I learned at a very early age that the sound of creaking stairs at night was definitely not a good sign. Once Dad reached the top of the stairs, I could hear his heavy breathing—the result of a dozen beers or a gallon of wine he easily drank in one day. It was as if he had to be drunk to beat us, and the drunker he was, the harder the beating. I could almost feel his hot breath near me as I lay in my bed on high alert, wondering whom he would choose as his next victim.

When I'd hear the first cry of pain coming from the boys' bedroom, I'd hide under my blankets and sigh with relief. He hadn't chosen me. Timmy was the unfortunate one again. I'd feel guilty about experiencing such relief, so I'd cover my ears to block out the cries. But I could still hear my brother's anguish as the leather strap, used for sharpening Dad's razor, came down on him once more. When the beating was over, I'd tiptoe to Timmy's bedside to see if he was all right. My heart broke each time I'd set eyes on his beaten, frail little body.

But my turn would arrive soon enough. Awakened by the feeling of blankets being ripped off me, my first reaction was to take a deep breath as the strap came down and blistered my skin to thick bloody welts. I never knew why Dad beat me. I only knew that Timmy and I served as a release for his frustration.

The creaking of stairs wasn't the only sound that kept us from falling into a deep sleep. The sound of dishes breaking, muffled screams, and pots and pans hitting the walls and floors were a good reason to stay awake. The noise at times made it impossible to know what was really going on. Now and again, curiosity would get the better of Timmy and me. We'd creep down the stairs, sit at the bottom, and lean against the closed door. This curiosity didn't pay at times. When the door would unexpectedly open wide, we'd fall to the kitchen floor. Being small and half asleep hindered our escape, and one of us would inevitably receive the last of Dad's fury.

One winter night, I awoke to what I thought was the howling of the wind. Half asleep and still unsure about what I was hearing, I stared at the bedroom window. The lace curtains were embedded in ice that had accumulated on the inside of the window. The faded picture of Jesus on the wall was a reminder of prayer.

The familiar sound of Dad's leather strap hitting flesh put me on high alert. A piercing cry from the boys' room sent me scurrying into the closet. I knew that sound. It was a unique cry, the last weak lamenting cry that finally satisfied dad's rage. Then total silence. Dad's heavy breathing penetrated my bedroom as he crept down the stairs. I held my breath until the sound of his snarling rage disappeared.

I went to Timmy's side. "Let's run away," I whispered.

Without saying a word, Timmy crawled out of bed and began to dress.

It was two in the morning. Dad had made beer, and the smell of hops and yeast filled the house. The copper boiler was stashed away in a dark cubbyhole in the girls' bedroom because it was the best place for the beer to ferment. The odor of fermenting beer that engulfed us gave us one more reason to run away.

We made sure we were well dressed for the freezing weather

outdoors. Timmy slipped into gray wool trousers and a jacket that Mom had made for him, black boots, and a wool hat, scarf, and mittens. I threw on navy blue trousers and jacket—also homemade by Mom—boots with fur at the top, a scarf, and a multicolored hat and matching mittens that Mom had knit from remnants of wool. Equipped with a few stolen cookies, Timmy and I tiptoed to the back of the house. We could hear the whistling of the wind through the cracks in the door. Timmy's eyes met my eager gaze, and we smiled as if to assure ourselves that it was the right thing to do.

The closest town was eighteen miles away, and the temperature was forty degrees below zero, but nothing would interfere with our escape. Even though it was dark and cold, and we didn't know how we were going to succeed, our plan still seemed possible. We wanted to get away from the smell of beer, from the hypocrisy, and from the anger that filled the house.
Daring yet alert, we opened the door and stepped outside. The frostiness in the air immediately hit our warm faces. We closed the door behind us and smiled as we walked away from the house, treading through drifting snow up to our knees. We were excited. We'd go far away and never see Dad again.

Minutes later, we stopped in our tracks when we noticed someone ahead of us. We peered through lashes already coated with a thin layer of ice. It was Dad! He asked us what we were doing. We stared at him, unable to speak. We stood facing him for the longest time. Tears froze to my face. Dad was speechless, as if he were having trouble choosing his victim. I supposed that finding himself face-to-face with both of us was too much for him to deal with. He couldn't decide. He probably preferred the surprise attacks at night when he couldn't see our faces.

Dad brought us back to the house and sent us to bed. I lay awake, wide-eyed, listening to every little noise in the house. I was particularly interested in the creaking of the stairs. Exhausted, I soon fell asleep. Nothing more happened that night.

The next morning, Timmy and I sat in the kitchen eyeing each other as if we had won this round. Maybe this time, we had.

#

Whenever Timmy and I snuck downstairs and saw Dad sprawled in his Laz-E-Boy recliner, so oblivious to his surroundings that his dentures were floating in his mouth, we knew nothing would wake him and off we'd run off into the woods.

The snow shone like crystals under the moon's path of light as Timmy and I sat side by side, bundled up from head to toe in our heavy winter clothing. Everything was so beautiful and quiet. Even the trees were sleeping. We spent hours pretending to count the stars and, before heading back home, we would wish:

Star light, star bright,
First star I see tonight.
Wish I may, wish I might
Get the wish I wish tonight.

Our wishes were secrets but, as we stared into each other's eyes, we knew they were identical.

Chapter 5
Best Things in Life

Living in the country offered more than its fair share of freebies. Nature frequently exceeded our expectations and provided delights that raised our spirits—no matter what season it was.

When the lake froze over in the winter, it provided our family with ice for the summer. The neighborhood men sawed the ice into huge blocks while we skated close by or slid down the snowy banks. Nellie, our workhorse, a ten-year-old Clydesdale, often waited so long for the men to load the sleigh that icicles formed on her mouth and nostrils.

My siblings and I especially looked forward to the ride back home. We were all rosy cheeks, cold hands and feet, smiles and giggles as we cuddled under wool blankets. These priceless memories are gathered in a drawer of my mind and come out whenever I need to temper the bad times with the good.

Winter came and went, and each spring we emerged with hope, shedding our heavy clothes and exposing new bruises: black, blue, red, and yellowish brown—the ones that were on the way out. The snow had melted and mischief filled the air again.

Spring was an aphrodisiac, and Timmy and I often stood on the back porch, breathing in the scent of pine, spruce, and other budding foliage. We made time for play even though our schedules were overflowing with strenuous chores. We played hopscotch and meticulously chose pretty pieces of colored glass from our collection of broken bottles.

Summer was the season of rejuvenation. We ran through endless fields and filled our lungs with the sweet smell of country air.

We picked bunches of wildflowers, brought them home, and proudly placed them in empty milk bottles. We never received an expression of thanks from Mom, but this didn't stop us from replenishing the bottles with fresh flowers as often as we wanted.

Picking berries was a respected ritual, and Timmy and I spent days gathering blueberries in anticipation of Mom's delicious dumplings. As the summer came to an end, a more difficult task—picking raspberries—awaited us. We climbed over remnants of dead tree trunks, struggled to get past sharp branches, and succumbed to bee stings just to gather the sweet red berries. At the end of the day, we emerged from the woods frazzled, our hair filled with twigs and leaves. Overtired and on the verge of being sick from having eaten too many berries, we walked the long distance back home. Regardless, we knew that our hard efforts would be rewarded. In the cold of winter, we would enjoy the taste of hot raspberry pies with ice cream and homemade jam.

On our afternoon scavenger hunts, we searched for treasures by the lake. At every chance, we ate the odd but tasty mint buds we found under beds of moss. We later discovered that these mints were bug eggs. We also learned that the precious nectar we squeezed from the grasshoppers was...well, I'd rather not remember.

One day, I visited the farm next door and watched as Simone's father sat on a small stool and milked the cows. I was standing at the barn door when he turned and squirted milk from the cow directly into my mouth. I laughed and tried to swallow every drop of the hot sweet liquid that came my way, although most of it ended up on my clothes. My visits became a summer ritual, three times a week. Simone never joined in because she hated warm milk. Going to school in town in the fall broke the routine, but I managed to visit the farm on weekends anyway.

As much as milk was plentiful, candies were rare. It meant stealing an empty beer bottle from Dad's huge collection. Timmy and I weren't certain if Dad counted the empties or not because he'd sample a few bottles as soon as the beer had brewed and rotate his collection, but it was a risk we were willing to take. If Dad didn't notice a bottle was missing, then it wasn't a major sin. But just to be sure, we moved the bottles around.

Timmy was eighteen months younger than I. Because we were shoeless by choice, the summer holidays allowed for the soles of our feet to thicken like cushions. We ran with ease through sand, stones, and bush. With well-padded feet, we often walked three miles barefoot into the closest village, but the reward was worth it. One of Dad's empty beer bottles earned us three cents, which meant we could buy nine candies. This odd number made it difficult to decide who got the ninth candy, so it was shared. I diligently checked its size in Timmy's mouth every minute or so to make sure he didn't get that extra suck.

One spring day, Timmy and I were on the run again. We had stolen another beer bottle and laughed as we ran down the gravel road toward the village. Timmy's eyes widened with excitement when he noticed a pack of *Juicy Fruit* gum that had obviously spent the winter under the snow. He picked it up. Its faded yellow wrapping still shimmered in the sun. He opened the pack of gum and offered me a stick.

I stepped back, refusing to take it. "Maybe you should try it first," I said. "Maybe it's poisoned or something."

Timmy had no problem in sampling the gum. Once I saw the pleased look on his face, I tasted a piece, too. We split the pack and kept the gum for months, sticking the same piece on the bedpost every night before we fell asleep.

If one thing remained constant, it was Timmy's love of chewing gum. Two years later, we were strolling down Main Street, glancing at the shop windows in town, when a man spit out a huge glob of gum right in front of us. Without a second thought, Timmy bent down, picked up the gum from the sidewalk, and put it in his mouth.

I was shocked. When Timmy offered me half, I told him it was out of the question.

"It's still good. It's *Juicy Fruit*, I can tell." His lips smacked together in enjoyment.

#

Since our family lived so far from the closest town, Timmy and I used to take the bus to school. The driver was a wonderful man named Maninbal who greeted us with a smile every weekday morning. When the end of summer approached and blueberries were plentiful, Maninbal often stopped the bus on the way home. He let us take a fifteen-minute break to fill our paper cups with berries. In exchange, we placed fruit, cookies, or other gifts from our lunches on the dashboard of the bus.

Nellie would always be waiting for me at the roadside—one of her many other jobs. Most important of all, she was my friend. She acted as a bridge when we played *London Bridge*. Whenever I had a secret to tell, I went to Nellie. Nellie listened.

I would grab hold of her long mane to mount her and off I rode, pretending to be a princess on a beautiful horse on my way to wonderland. Nellie wasn't as elegant as a racehorse. She had rough hair and a tired look about her. But when I rode her, she felt like a thoroughbred. I imagined she had wings as she galloped through the trails, three miles into the bush to a lumberjack camp.

The lumberjacks were huge gentle giants in plaid shirts whose hearts were as visible as their powerful muscles. I didn't know their names, but I felt safe around them. What was lacking in the way of closeness with my parents, I found to a degree with the lumberjacks.

Every day after school, the cook—a short, pudgy, bald man who smiled a lot and reminded me of an elf—had a piece of pie or cake for me and an apple for Nellie. He called me his little fart. I sat at the rough wooden table with the giants who emanated a body odor so strong that it often made my nose twitch. Regardless, the trip was the highlight of my day. I felt as if I were in fairyland. I was a tiny girl, riding a magical horse, living among tall bearded giants. I felt so secure.

Nellie seemed to gallop faster on the way home. At times she raced so fast into the stable that, if my timing were a bit off, I'd hit the side of the stable and fall to the ground. I sat in pain at the dinner table yet smiled at the memory of the great dessert I had just eaten. Secrets were kept like precious jewels never to be revealed. Most of all, I didn't want to jeopardize my friendship with the gentle giants.

I eventually let Timmy in on my secret. I trusted him. One weekend, we hitched Nellie to a cart and rode together to the camp deep in the woods. We chatted with the cook who fed us dessert to our hearts' content. Timmy had never enjoyed so much attention. He often thanked me for sharing my secret with him and never told a soul.

Chapter 6
Jekyll and Hyde

Mom was a loving mother and a gentle woman, but wanted everyone to think she was a martyr. She desperately wanted to be seen as an image of perfection. She thought she had succeeded in reflecting this image, but many could see behind the veil. Mom was a prude.

She was a schoolteacher and had made the mistake of marrying a carpenter. She sometimes wondered what it would have been like to have married a prominent man instead. As a result, she often belittled Dad for not having chosen a more prestigious profession. In her eyes, he was never important enough. He was just a thin, vile-tempered man who worked hard to keep a roof over our heads, keep us warm, feed us, and beat us.

To compensate, Mom associated with doctors, lawyers, and priests in her make-believe world of upper society, especially if it meant attracting attention in any way possible. Mom's intense need for attention was triggered by her belief that Dad's status in society wasn't adequate. She prayed every day, tried to make Dad a better person, went to confession frequently, and kept her image of a martyr untarnished. She took aspirins every day, claiming it was a preventative for anything and everything she might catch. She also liked brandy. These two remedies didn't mix well, as she eventually discovered. She tried to keep her secrets deeply embedded so as not to reveal them, yet she was unaware that they were so transparent.

On better days, Mom was gifted in making her stories believable—especially to Dad. She was fussy about food and succeeded in convincing him that the only meat she was able to eat was steak and roast ham. However, hamburger served in various ways was the main meal for the rest of us. Mom's "special diet" was a mystery to us, but Dad made sure she never ran out of her favorite foods. I found this odd because I knew how strict Dad was about spending money.

As for Dad … well, he probably wondered how different his life would have been if his first wife hadn't passed away. I was convinced that he had married the wrong woman when he chose Mom. If he had married a woman who would have made him feel important or loved him just a bit, his life would have turned out quite differently. Maybe he would have been less violent. I supposed he had a mean streak because he had never experienced love at a young age and later ran into situations he couldn't begin to understand. It was as if he had been born with a tag around his neck that read, "Never going to make it," in bold letters.

Dad had beautiful dark blue eyes, but they were so cold. When he was happy, no one could tell because he didn't express his emotions. It was as if a barrier from his heart to his eyes prevented joy or sadness to surface. But I knew he had feelings. I had been blessed to see them surface once or twice, which convinced me that he had a heart. It was a damaged heart, but even so, he had one. Any visible moments of genuine affection on his part gave me the gift of forgiveness at an early age, and I thank him for that.

Although Dad was master of his home, he lacked self-esteem at times. I eventually understood that the anger he lashed out at us was also a reflection of his own insecurity and pain. He released his rage in the only way he knew: through physical means. As a short man, he chose to beat his wife and children and fill their days with fear. This fear was constant, like a shadow hiding behind our laughter, and we were always on guard.

Dad was very conscious about his thinning hair, yet he proudly went to the barbershop every month. He never understood why the barber refused to take into consideration the little amount of hair he had and charged him the same price for a cut as everyone else. This fact infuriated Dad and gave him another reason to flare up.

One night, moonlight shone into my room as the strap came down on me, over and over. I caught a glimpse beyond Dad's teary blue eyes, behind the rage and control, behind the release that he seemed to get as the sound of the leather strap hit my skin. I saw desperation, but I also saw love blocked out by the intensity of his anger. I knew it was there. It just couldn't surface because it was a feeling he had never experienced before. If Dad could have moved past the rage that engulfed his every thought, I think he would have found life more endurable. He was the unhappiest person I have ever known.

As contradictions went, Dad would have loved to be a doctor. Every time we bruised, cut, scraped, or burned ourselves, he was there to help us. Mom had a hard time fixing scrapes and cuts, so when it was serious, Dad was the one we wanted.

On the stump beside a pile of wood at the back of the house was an axe. I often went out and chopped wood for the cold winter ahead, lifting the axe high into the air and slamming it down, over and over. My brother Timmy and I became experts in chopping and piling wood. The work got done and that was what counted.

I was chopping wood one day to make a knife and an arrow. A serious game of cowboys and Indians was brewing in the air. I lifted the heavy axe as I had done many times before, but it slipped and sliced into my right index finger. I held my bleeding finger and ran home screaming.

Dad rushed into the kitchen, opened the medicine cabinet, and reached for the cure-all: iodine. He sat me on the kitchen counter, opened the wound, and poured the iodine in. Deaf ears ignored the familiar sound of my screams, but soon the pain grew less intense. After Dad skillfully wrapped my finger, I ran outside and continued with my plans. It was a good day because I had had Dad near me and he had been gentle—for a change. The only reminder I have today of that accident is a scar that has faded with the years.

Timmy and I were chasing each other again and running barefoot in the fields when I had another accident. A piece of wood with a rusted quarter-inch nail facing upward lay hidden among the tall grasses. As my foot slammed down on the nail, I let out the loudest scream. Timmy helped me hop home as I screeched in pain, terrified at the sight of the plank still attached to my foot.

Dad opened the front door and immediately placed me face down on the counter by the sink. He grabbed the piece of wood and slowly pulled it from my foot. He opened the wound with tweezers, poured in the iodine, and stuffed the gap with gauze. I held my breath for the longest time, then exhaled with a scream so loud that I gave myself goose bumps. After Dad had carefully placed the last piece of tape over the wound, a momentary expression of pride and satisfaction spread over his face.

We tried to hide toothaches from Dad for fear he'd practice his dental skills on us. Keeping teeth as long as possible wasn't a priority for Dad, not to mention that he just didn't have the two dollars to pay a dentist for pulling out a tooth. On one occasion, I was determined to hide my pain, but the swelling of my cheek caused by an abscess gave me away, and Dad led me down the steps to the basement.

I held my mouth wide open while Dad tried unsuccessfully to get a good grip on my tooth, but the pliers kept slipping, sending shockwaves of pain through my head. The pain at times was so intense that I froze to the chair and was unable to make a sound. Anger and foul words raced through my mind, and after the pain had subsided, I knew another sin had been added to my list for confession.

The oddest thing about Dad's "amateur" healing techniques is that I never caught an infection from any accident I had. Dad made sure of it.

So, Mom, it was there all the time, but you just didn't notice it. Dad had talent, but you didn't allow yourself to see it. In your eyes, his talents were camouflaged by the absence of papers that would validate his knowledge. In your eyes, he was just a carpenter.

Although Dad hadn't gone to school, except for a few years when he was young, he was self-taught. English literature was one of his favorite subjects, and history and geography. His knowledge of these subjects was exceptional and his memory even better. He insisted that we speak English correctly and use the right terms while conversing.

As for me, I wasn't interested in what had happened hundreds of years ago. I was interested in today. I liked the challenge of numbers, and I loved literature. I memorized Shakespeare's *Merchant of Venice, Hamlet, Macbeth*, and *Anthony and Cleopatra.* Pretending to be the characters made it easy to remember.

My friend June came over to the house one day. It was the first time she had met Dad. "How are *youse* guys?" she said.

The word *youse* sent Dad's head into a spin. He sat us side by side and gave us a speech on the English language. *Youse* wasn't a word, he said, and his ears were never to hear that word again, especially not in his house. June started to laugh but stopped when she saw how Dad was staring at her.

"What's wrong with your Dad?" she asked me as she was leaving.

"Nothing, don't worry. He's tired, I guess. Just don't say that word again," I warned her.

Rarely did any of my friends return to the house a second time. Even though they didn't admit it, Dad had scared them off. The only friend who did drop by again said she preferred to stay outside on the porch.

Dad's fixation with doing things the right way extended beyond language. He took great pride in washing the clothes. The sheets were so white that, when the sun shone on them, the blinding effect was similar to sunshine hitting snow on a clear crisp winter day. The neighbors often commented on the brightness of the clothes, which made Dad sigh with satisfaction every time.

Because Mom and Dad didn't own a car, they did their shopping either with a neighbor or by taxi. One day, Dad hitched a ride to town for groceries but couldn't afford a taxi back home. He held two large paper bags filled with cans and stood at the town exit, hoping someone would offer him a ride.

A few cars went by but nobody stopped for him, so he walked eighteen miles back home. As he entered the house, he placed the bags on the kitchen table and smiled. His blue eyes shone proudly out of a weather-beaten face. Timmy and I noticed the large protruding veins on his thin, tanned arms, but Mom showed neither appreciation nor sympathy for Dad that day.

Dad later bought an old bike and cycled to town. One day, the bike went missing. I overheard Dad tell Mom he had given it to the milkman in exchange for milk for the children. Although Dad had a bad temper and couldn't understand acts of affection, I appreciated how relentless he was in providing for his family.

Dad's diligence in doing chores extended to Timmy and me but with severity as an added factor. Our tasks were especially difficult in the winter when snow fell in abundance. One storm in particular lasted for days. High drifts blocked the path to the ice in the woodshed, so we dug a tunnel through the snow to get to it. With the help of our homemade sleds painted bright red, Timmy and I transported wood back to the house.

I was laughing with my brother as we pulled the sleds. I called out to him, "Timmy, I'll race you under the bridge. The loser is a rotten egg."

Suddenly, a hand gripped my jacket, lifted me in the air, and threw me to the ground. It was Dad. He stuffed my mouth with snow and asked me to repeat what I had just said.

"I wanted to race with Timmy under the bridge," I answered.

Again, wrong answer. Dad sat on me, stuffed snow in my mouth, and rubbed it in my face with all the strength a mad little man could gather when his temper exploded. He wanted me to give him the answer he was looking for, but I had no idea what it was.

Again, I cried out, "I just wanted to get wood. I just wanted to race under the bridge."

Dad lost control. He opened my jacket and, in a rage, stuffed as much snow down my chest, into my face and ears, and on any open area he could find, hitting and asking me over and over what I had said. All the while, Timmy stood rooted, unable to help.

The commotion drew Nanette's attention. She peeked out the door, listened to what was going on, and yelled out to me. "Say, 'through the tunnel, Diana.' Say, 'through the tunnel'."

By this time, Timmy had caught on. He yelled the word tunnel as loud as he could.

"Tunnel!" I shouted. "Tunnel!"

Dad instantly snapped out of his frenzy. He dropped me like a hot potato and ordered that we go on with our chores. My brother and I sobbed together as we finished bringing in the wood.

Then came the piling of the wood. It had to be piled in a specific manner to prevent the cords of wood from falling. Timmy and I knew how to pile the wood properly because an expert had taught us.

From time to time, Dad would inspect our work. He'd deliberately sway the cords until they fell to the ground, then he'd stare at us with cold blue eyes and say nothing. Neither Timmy nor I would dare to speak. Answering back a parent was forbidden because it went against one of the rules on the sin list. So we'd start piling the wood again, stopping only when our work was finished and Dad was satisfied with the results. We'd go straight to bed, not having the energy to worry that our sleep might be interrupted.

There were no good mornings or good nights. God forbid, we'd have a good night's sleep. Although physical scars faded over time and left faint shadows, mental scars created lasting impressions. Every evening, as we got ready for bed, fear swelled in our hearts and minds. We would re-energize ourselves the following day, filling our lungs with fresh air and our hearts with hope.

Chapter 7
Close Calls

Because Mom had contacts with the right sort of people, we were privileged and spent a good part of each summer at a cottage near a lake. The water was as cold as ice, but it didn't prevent us from swimming and playing all day long. Water fights were common. Nanette and I would head out in a canoe. Moments later, the boys who lived next door would catch up to us. Their goal was to throw us out of the canoe and steal it from us, and they succeeded often enough. But we were great swimmers, and we played where the current was at its fiercest and the water at its deepest. We weren't afraid. We would become one with the water.

A trick we often played on Mom was to hide in overblown tire tubes. From the cottage window, all she could see were the tire tubes. She'd panic, thinking that one of us had drowned. I realized later that we shouldn't have played such a cruel joke on her.

A sitter arrived at the cottage one night because my parents were going out—a rare event. The sitter was fifteen—about two years older than Nanette and four years older than me. Mom and Dad warned us that we weren't allowed to go swimming after dinner. Everyone agreed to obey.

But after dinner, the sitter decided she wanted to go for a swim anyway. What she didn't know was that the bottom of the lake dipped fifteen feet just steps from the dock. She waded into the cold water and lost her breath, took a few steps forward, and slipped under the water. When we saw her arms flailing, we knew she was drowning.

Nanette instantly jumped in and tried to grab her. The

desperate sitter clung onto my sister's waist and began to drag her down.

Timmy and I stood on the dock, screaming for help as we watched the two girls sink deeper and deeper into the dark water. My sister must have kicked her or pushed her away because the sitter lost her grip on her. Nannette came up for a breath of air and then dove back in to rescue the sitter.

The neighbors had heard our screams and were now standing next to us on the dock. We were never as grateful as when we saw Nanette drag the sitter to shore. With everyone's attention focused on the sitter, no one knew the drastic state Nanette was in until a neighbor turned and noticed her sitting at the end of the dock. She was cold, pale, and trembling, and in an obvious state of shock.

The neighbor helped Nanette up and led her to the cottage. I noticed a hint of satisfaction in my sister's bloodshot eyes, but I also detected an overwhelming fear that came with the realization she had touched the edge of death.

Weeks passed before Nanette could grasp the magnitude of her bravery. I can't imagine what my life would have been like had I lost my sister, my best friend.

#

Since we needed ice to keep our food fresh in the icebox, trips across the bay were a weekly obligation. One night, Mom and I slowly paddled our way back to the cottage in a canoe filled with blocks of ice. The stars and moon were partially hidden behind clouds, so we had to strain our eyes to make sure we didn't wander too far from shore. The weight of the ice caused the canoe to sink lower so that it was only a few inches above the water level. But we weren't worried. We had often completed the same task before. Only this time, something went wrong.

I heard a splash. Mom was gone! She had fallen over the edge of the canoe, and I couldn't see her anywhere. I heard a thump on the bottom of the canoe. I figured it was Mom. Thump, thump, again. I screamed out for help in the dark. I looked around and noticed dim lights in the cottages that surrounded the bay, but no one came running to help us.

I sunk my hands into the water and frantically searched for Mom. I grabbed onto what I thought was a handful of weeds, but it was her hair! I was pulling and screaming when I heard Mom cough. I was afraid that the canoe might tip over but happy that she was all right. I helped her get back in. "What happened, Mom?"

Her response was calm and simple. "My oar got stuck. I fell in, and I can't swim."

Because of that major scare, I avoided ice trips for the rest of the summer, and Mom went with one of my siblings instead.

#

Back at home, the hottest season of the year offered us lots of occasions for mischief. One day, I spotted a wasp's nest. I dared Timmy to climb up the tree and stick a twig into the nest. Without a moment's hesitation, he crawled up. Wasps began to swirl around him, so I thought it might be a good idea to get a head start. I ran as fast as I could, then I heard a horrible scream. I turned around to see Timmy running for his life. The wasps had aligned their way to his tiny shoulder. Once we arrived home, I had to force myself not to laugh. His shoulder had doubled in size. My parents didn't seem concerned in the least and had a hearty laugh out of it too. Timmy and I kept away from wasp nests from then on but found other naughty tricks to play on each other.

Our quest for adventure took us to other points of interest. A fire tower that stood on a nearby hilltop attracted our attention. Timmy and I felt daring and made a bet on who could climb to the top first. In the next moment, we were racing up the tower.

Halfway from the top, I decided to look down. My stomach tightened, and I felt dizzy. I couldn't move. I wouldn't move. I welded myself to the tower.

Timmy begged me to come down, but I wasn't going anywhere. He couldn't convince me to budge, so he frantically screamed for help. We later found out that a watchman in the tower had called for help.

Soon two firemen were climbing the tower. They approached me, yet their voices seemed far away. Fear had overpowered me, and I couldn't see clearly, but I sensed that the firemen were trying to release my grip. I was determined not to let them do it.

All of a sudden, I felt my hand move away from the tower. I don't remember the trip down, but I do remember that the moment my foot touched the ground, I took off like a wild animal. "Thank you," I yelled out as I ran down the hill. "Thank you."

I was even more grateful that Dad never found out.

Chapter 8
Sins of Affection

Visitors were scarce. Yet I dreaded the thought of someone coming over to our home because Dad would do his usual thing: take out a picture of me at the age of three, standing naked next to a baby carriage and wearing only a heavy khaki helmet. Dad and the visitors would laugh hysterically, their beady eyes glancing back and forth from the picture to me as if they were visualizing me naked. In a rage, I attempted to retrieve the picture and was successful many times, but there was always another one.

My parents' bedroom was off limits to the children, but at fifteen, I dared to search it. I found another of those pictures. I remember tearing it into little pieces and crying for the longest time over the years of humiliation I had endured. I never did see another picture.

Dad wasn't the only one who liked to draw attention to his children. Mom felt she had to impress and convince everyone who came to the house that she had a happy, organized, and obedient family. Every time we had guests over, she stood Nanette and me side by side. "Sing for the visitors, girls," she'd say as she sat at the piano and played.

"East is East and West is West," Nanette and I sang like shy little puppets, swinging our arms left and right, as we ran through a chorus of "Buttons and Bows." Although we didn't feel like singing at times, we didn't dare disobey Mom. It would have gone against one of the major sins on the list.

Good Friday was another singing day for us. Mom made hot cross buns. We sat at the breakfast nook and sang "The Old Rugged Cross" in a sad voice. We loved this day. Because we had fasted from desserts for the last forty days, we were now allowed to eat the delicious buns. I had once suggested that Dad fast also. My other suggestion was that he put away his leather strap for forty days. He didn't find it amusing. He was proud of his strap, and it would never leave its place on the hook behind the washroom door.

Christmas was an exciting time in our lives. Every year, we spent hours browsing through the pages of the Simpson Sears catalog as we prepared our Christmas list. We wrote down every item we wanted and indicated the page, the price, and a thorough description to avoid any errors. Once more, the household would turn into a robotic scene as Mom sat at the piano and played Christmas carols while her little puppets sang to the music. Anyone peeking through the window might have envied the perfect family scene we portrayed.

On Christmas Eve, we were delighted with gifts of homemade clothes and fresh oranges but disappointed when, as usual, we didn't get anything on the list. One year in particular was especially hard for Timmy. Ever since he was a young boy, he had asked for a red sled for Christmas. When it was time to open our presents, Timmy's eyes lit up as when he saw a red sled under the tree. Dad reached for the sled he had made himself and handed it to Billy instead. The only time Timmy was allowed to use it was for his chores, like transporting wood from the shed.

I wasn't surprised. Once I had asked Mom to pay for piano lessons but she had refused. She insisted though, that Billy take them instead. He had hated every minute of it.

Early Christmas morning, we would go to mass and pray that, maybe next year, something on the list might come our way. At fifteen, I asked for a pink dog to stuff my pajamas in. I actually received it. I still had it when I got married.

Chapter 9
Sins of the Father

Excitement was intense when we heard the news that we were moving, house and all, to town. We did our homework at the kitchen table and admired the scenery that moved by in slow motion as the house crept along the eighteen-mile gravel road. The drivers were pleased when Mom invited them to feast on her famous raspberry pie, which made Dad smile proudly.

The first thought that crossed my mind was relief that we would be surrounded by neighbors. I was convinced that our lives would change for the better. As soon as the house was sitting on the foundation, I began to search the streets for friends.

Timmy, on the other hand, was shy and lacked self-confidence. His eyes always had a sad look about them. He was afraid of rejection, so he cocooned himself even more and never made friends. Because of his fear of Dad and his mistrust in everyone, he didn't ask questions and learned most things on his own, which kept him busy but not necessarily in the best of ways. When he wanted something, he would steal it. Nothing was a sin for him. His definition of life was "to each, his own."

One day, another fire broke out in the huge copper boiler that Dad stashed in my bedroom closet. Billy, my younger brother, hated shoes as much as I did and thought it would be a good idea to set fire to all the shoes he could find. So he did.

Later he sat at the breakfast nook and watched as his siblings twitched their noses, sniffing the air at the smell of smoke. Panic struck like lightening as we all rushed from the house, except Billy—

the arsonist. He stayed seated because he knew where the smoke was coming from. He was probably wishing the shoes would have time to disintegrate.

A scolding was the best punishment Dad could think of, although Timmy and I agreed it might be appropriate that he use the famous leather strap. Our idea was based on wishful thinking since Dad's rage was never released on any other than Timmy and me.

#

Dad always prepared lunch for us. While we were eating our sandwiches one afternoon, my siblings and I noticed frustration building up in Dad. He was on the verge of another angry outburst. Who would he chose as his victim this time?

Young Timmy became his target once again. Dad literally picked him up and threw him down the basement stairs. Timmy's feet never touched the ground before he landed on the cement floor. Dad stood at the top of the stairs, daring him to come back upstairs. Timmy did. He slowly started up the stairs, but Dad kicked him as he approached the top landing. Motionless for a few moments, Timmy stood up and started up the stairs again. Dad kicked him again, sending him flying backwards down the stairs onto the cement floor one more time. Our screams and pleads couldn't stop Dad, and Mom stayed back.

Dad stood there, eyes blazing, as if to dare Timmy to try again, but Timmy wasn't moving. Dad ran down the stairs. We thought he was feeling remorseful and was going to pick him up. Instead, Dad pulled Timmy to his feet and began banging his head against the cement wall. My brother seemed lifeless. He didn't utter a single sound during the whole ordeal. Dad then sent us to our rooms.

The night was long and sleepless. We were on high alert. We listened for any sound that might suggest that a storm was brewing in Dad's head again. But nothing happened.

The next morning, I was surprised to see Timmy sitting at the breakfast nook. His small body was covered with bruises. As I watched the tears well up in his big blue eyes and roll down his cheeks, my heart broke. We later decided that we'd try to run away again. We'd wait until Dad fell asleep and make our escape that very night. We were older and had acquired new skills. We were convinced that together we could make it.

But Dad knew better than to go to bed after he had seen Timmy and me whispering in a corner. He knew we were up to something. My brother and I took turns sneaking downstairs for a glass of water and were surprised to find Dad asleep at the table in the breakfast nook. Even while he was sleeping, he gave me the creeps. Timmy and I canceled our plans and agreed that we should wait a bit longer.

Over the years, Timmy and I grew tougher. It wasn't because the beatings didn't hurt; it was because we could endure them better. We could hold back the tears a little longer each time. We soon realized that this wasn't such a great idea because the beatings would continue until we gave in, until Dad heard our last faint cries of desperation. Only then would he let go.

After Dad died, Timmy told me how angry the beatings had made him. But to my surprise, my brother had formed a plan. He would sleep with a pillow over his bottom in case his turn came up. So every time Dad would hit him with the strap, Timmy would pretend to scream out in pain. Satisfied with the results, Dad would go back downstairs, and Timmy would hide his face in the pillow and laugh.

#

I eyed the bowl of mushroom soup that Dad had put in front of me at lunchtime one day. I couldn't eat it. Just the sight of it made me feel sick. Everyone else had finished their soup except me. Then Nanette called out for help with the dishes.

"I'll go help you when I'm ready," I abruptly answered, my eyes still glaring at my bowl of soup. No sooner were the words out of my mouth, I realized I had broken the rule of answering back.

Within seconds, Dad headed straight toward me. I pushed myself out of the breakfast nook and laughed as I ran around and around the table with Dad in hot pursuit. His face was red with fury, his lips seemed to be covered with a thick white coating, and his eyes were deep blue. The familiar contrasts in color told me that I was in trouble. Dad was in a frenzied rage and out of control. I would soon be at his mercy.

He caught up to me and threw me to the floor. He grabbed his weapon of choice: a huge piece of firewood. He kicked me and pounded my ribs and stomach with the piece of wood until I fainted.

When I regained consciousness, I saw my mother pointing toward the stairway. I was relieved that that she was sending me to my room.

But Dad had a better idea: I would go to school and remember to never answer back again. So I changed my clothes and put on a long-sleeved blouse to hide the bruises. I ran to school, not stopping to talk to friends.

Class began, and our project that day was water painting on glass. Within minutes after the teacher had left the room, a mischievous student walked up to me, painted two red lines on my face, and called me a squaw.

Anger surged through my bruised ninety-pound body. I grabbed the boy by the collar and the crotch of his pants and flung him over two rows of seats. He landed face first on the corner of a desk.

I froze. I couldn't believe what had happened. I had lost control–just like Dad.

Everyone stood still, their expressions displaying anger and disbelief.

Moments later, the teacher returned. The classroom was buzzing with excitement because students wanted to give him their version of what had happened. The boy I had thrown was sitting on the ground, dazed and bleeding profusely. Someone brought him to the hospital, and I found out later that he had suffered multiple fractures on his nose.

The teacher stood at the front of the class and stared at me in amazement. My violent conduct wasn't the usual behavior of a shy fourteen-year-old. I didn't say a word as tears ran down my cheeks and trickled red drops onto my painting. After the teacher had restored order to the class, the students went back to working on their water paintings in silence. Soon class was dismissed, and everyone left except me.

The teacher took a seat facing me. He put my hands in his and asked me what had happened. I was still in shock, but the teacher's comforting voice brought me back to reality. I began to cry. I knew that no one could possibly understand the rage and pain festering inside me. I wanted to explain the reason for my outburst, but I had a hard time understanding it myself. Worst of all, I would have had to tell him about my father, and I could never do that. I stood up, reassured the professor that I was fine, and told him that I had to hurry home.

My actions that day triggered unexpected reactions from the other students. The girls smiled reluctantly, then whispered behind my back when they thought I wasn't looking. The boys would run away from me, pretending to be afraid. Their actions made me regret what I had done to my classmate even more.

Daily tension at the kitchen table persisted for years. It was no surprise that my constant alertness to changes in Dad's humor and the fear of his flare-ups triggered health problems in me at a young age. My body's normal process of gastric gases was constantly interrupted, causing me to feel nauseous. To rectify the situation, I would search my parent's bedroom for the bottle of ENO fruit salt. It soon became an addiction.

Like my body, my mind was constantly on the defensive. Should I or shouldn't I? Was it a sin? Was it possible that I was sinning while I was praying? Yes, it was. I prayed: *Dear God, please make Dad die. Please take him away. He isn't happy and neither are we. I promise I will be good, and I will not commit another sin the rest of my life. Please make Dad die.*

I fervently said this prayer every night. When I had finished, I'd tiptoe downstairs, listen at Dad's bedroom door, and hope that God had heard my prayer. I'd jump up in fright whenever Dad's loud snore reached my ears. Disappointed, I'd return to my room and drop to my knees again. *Dear God....*

I never understood what provoked Dad's fits of rage or how he could choose which child he wanted to abuse. There was no logic behind his reasoning, unless dark secrets lurked in his past. All I knew was that, out of five children, Timmy or I always seemed to be in the wrong place at the wrong time. Because we were the targets of Dad's beatings, we began to hate the other siblings for getting off easy. We often wondered what we had done wrong and how we could remedy the situation. We never did find out.

Chapter 10
Money Can't Buy

Living close to our neighbors had its advantages. Fresh carrots were in abundance and came from their gardens. At dusk, when dares filled the air, Timmy and I would jump fences and raid their backyards. Fence jumping wasn't a problem for skinny kids. Once we grabbed a handful of carrots, we hid behind a fence. We sat and ate carrots that still smelled of earth—a reward well deserved. The fact that the lady we were stealing from wasn't too friendly served as the logic behind our sin, so we classified it as a minor sin. We stole the carrots with little remorse because we believed that a quick confession would clear us of all guilt, until the next carrot craving overpowered us.

Every Sunday, we went to mass at the nearby church. As the parishioners were reciting the Apostles' Creed out loud, my five-year-old sister joined in. Sissy was proud to know this prayer by heart. "Born of the Virgin Mary and punch the pilot" were her words.

I looked at her and smiled. I wasn't sure I had heard right.

The following Sunday, there it was again: "Born of the Virgin Mary and punch the pilot" instead of "suffered under Pontius Pilot." This incident would often give us a chuckle or two.

But laughter was rare in our house. One early Sunday morning, after arguments and screams had interrupted our sleep throughout the night, Timmy and I walked into the kitchen. Dad was sitting at the breakfast nook, his face in his hands. The sound of his labored breathing sent chills up and down my spine. Mom was silently puttering around the kitchen sink. She was desperately trying to tell us something with her eyes, but fear hid any hint about the message.

"Hurry kids, go to mass," Dad said, never lifting his head.

Mom's reaction was a nod to indicate that we should obey. I sensed a familiar uneasiness in the air and knew that she was about to suffer at Dad's hand. What were they arguing about this time? What was the cause of all the hatred? Whatever it was, I was convinced it would end in extreme mental and physical pain for Mom.

Nanette, Billy, and Sissy were quiet during mass, but Timmy and I paid little attention to the preacher. Eager for the service to end, we kept glancing at the church doors. The priest lifted his hand to bless the congregation, and before he had time to make the sign of the cross and say, "Go in peace," Timmy and I were out the door and halfway home.

"Where's Mom?" Timmy asked as he rushed into the house.

Dad was leaning against the kitchen sink, head bent, motionless except for his heavy breathing.

But Timmy and I knew what had happened. We could hear faint whimpering from our parents' bedroom. I stood facing Dad and silently wished for answers. Then Dad lifted his head and stared directly into my eyes. His dark blue glare revealed uncontrollable rage, pain, hatred, and sorrow, but no tears.

The rest of the day was uneventful. Timmy and I ran through the fields but kept an eye on the house in the hope of catching a glimpse of Mom. But she never surfaced.

Dad made shepherd's pie that evening. We ate our dinner in silence and didn't dare make eye contact with him as he sat at the table with us, drowning his anguish in homemade beer.

The next morning, Mom was sitting at the kitchen table. Her face was masked with heavy makeup, which only accentuated the black bruises and cuts. She stared at us through bloodshot eyes. Because Dad was watching, we restrained our emotions.

After Dad had fallen asleep in his recliner, Timmy whispered, "Mom! Come with us. Let's run away."

Mom had difficulty holding back the tears. She smiled and said, "One day, one day."

"We can work, Mom. We can chop wood and clean houses," I tried to persuade her as I yanked on her arm.

"You're still too young. Wait until you're at least sixteen," she said, her voice calm.

"Seven years is a long time, Mom," Timmy cried out. "It's too long."

The following Sunday, Timmy stole a nickel from Dad and decided to ask God for help. We stood at the front of the church and stared at the rows of unlit candles. Timmy put the nickel in the slot and lit a candle.

"He'll never see this flicker," he said to me. "I need to make Him see my request, but I only have one nickel." Timmy lit two more candles and waited. No one was paying attention to him, so he continued to light more candles. "Can you see the twelve candles now, God?" Timmy knelt beside me and whispered, "I don't think God will mind if I only paid for one. What's more important is that He needs to be able to see them."

God never answered Timmy's prayer. The pain and brutality my brother suffered over time caused him to slowly cut off any bond that might anchor him to the family. Because he had never experienced love or affection, his relentless search for ways to buy love soon became apparent and intensified through the years. He looked in back alleys, behind churches, and in jacket pockets that were unattended. He brought home anything of interest to Dad in the hope that he might approve and be more lenient toward him. But the stolen gifts did nothing to control Dad's temper when he became angry.

As the smell of spring and scented blossoms filled the air, Timmy's senses grew hungry for new experiences. He began his hunt for hidden treasures. The ground behind a church where bingo was held on Saturday nights was one of his preferred spots for finding money. One evening, Timmy noticed an object sitting on a pile of snow. A frozen turkey, still fully wrapped, turned out to be the jackpot of the evening. He hurried home, ran into the house, and offered the turkey to Dad. Without a word, Dad took it from him and thawed it out. We feasted the following day, but Dad never whispered a word of thanks to Timmy.

#

When I was twelve years old, I had a job. I helped three children with their homework, gave them their baths, and cooked dinner for them every evening. I also washed the dishes and floors, and did the laundry and ironing. I received seven dollars a week to work five days a week after school and on weekends.

Every week, I gave the money to my father, hoping that he might be more merciful toward me when he'd burst into one of his rages. But I should have learned from experience. Compassion eluded his mind whenever he was at his best—in control.

I loved to window-shop but could never afford the fashionable clothing displayed in the stores. One day, a skirt in a store window caught my attention. I had to have it. When I arrived home, I took my mother aside and told her about the skirt I had seen. I couldn't tell if she was listening to me or not. She seemed annoyed as I blabbered on and on but finally decided to go to the store with me.

I tried to make a deal with her. I offered to give her my pay of seven dollars a week if she would buy the skirt. "Please, Mom, will you buy it for me? I'll pay you back."

She said nothing. As we walked back home, her reaction was less than enthusiastic. I couldn't tell what she was thinking about or if she had even heard what I had said.

A week later, my dream was crushed when I saw Nanette wearing the same skirt I had asked Mom to buy for me. I looked at Mom in disbelief and ran out of the house into the pouring rain. I sat on the curb until I was drenched.

I hated Mom for what she had done. I was sorry I had ever mentioned the skirt to her. As I sat on the curb wading my feet in a puddle of water, I wondered if aliens really existed and hoped that if they did, they would see me and take me away.

Chapter 11
Sexual Innocence

At sixteen, my friends had developed into pretty young girls who were crazy about boys, whereas I had hit a maturity roadblock at the age of twelve. I had yet to find a boy that I found attractive.

That summer, I worked at Beaver Lumber as a receptionist. I still kept my part-time job and handed over my weekly salary of seven dollars to my father but daydreamed about what I'd buy with my first full-time paycheck. Everything in the department store was so beautiful. I wanted it all but settled for a royal blue matching skirt and sweater.

Mom seemed unimpressed with my first purchase, but Nanette thought it was a great buy and tried it on. I couldn't help but notice how her curvaceous body filled the clothes. After she wore the outfit a few times, it became officially mine, and no one could take it away from me.

One day at work, a salesman walked up to me and asked if I'd like to go see a movie with him. I was surprised that a man in his thirties would be interested in taking me out, let alone a man who wore a suit and strong after-shave lotion. I called Mom to ask for her permission. She agreed without hesitation.

I told the salesman that I had to be home by nine. Disappointment crossed his face, and I could almost hear the calculator working in his head. I thought he was going to ask me if I were kidding, but then he said he'd pick me up at six-thirty.

The theater seemed enormous as I took a seat next to him. The scent of his after-shave was still strong, but I ignored it because I was so eager to see my first movie in a real theater. But an hour into the movie, my date seemed agitated. "What's wrong?" I asked.

"I already saw this movie. I think we should leave." He gave me a stern look.

I felt as if I had to obey. I knew he was frustrated with me because every time he put his arm around me, I stood up and stared at him, questioning his move. He smiled and withdrew his arm, but just for a few moments.

"How does the movie end?" I asked him as we left the theater.

He didn't answer.

"That's fine," I said. "Now you can bring me home."

He started the ignition and headed in the wrong direction.

I immediately panicked. "You're going the wrong way!"

I tried to open the car door but he pulled me toward him. "I just want to drive around a bit. I'll take you home by nine, don't worry."

I wondered what I was so nervous about. After all, he worked at the same place as I did. I sat back and tried to enjoy the ride.

He drove to a place called Lovers' Lane and stopped the car.

"Why did you stop here?" I asked.

"Don't worry. My car stops sometimes, but it will restart in a few minutes."

Something didn't feel right. "Forget it. I can walk home." As I turned to open the door, he grabbed me. He pulled me toward him and smothered me with tongue-twisting, saliva-exchanging kisses. I tried to push him away, but he was too strong. All of a sudden, he began to tremble.

On the school bus, I had once seen a young man foaming at the mouth while he was having an epileptic seizure. It had scared me, and I thought this man was having a seizure too. I was terrified and asked him what I could do to help. He didn't answer. I screamed for help, but there was no one around. "You're scaring me," I cried. "You're doing the same thing a boy did on a bus. I don't know what to do. Please stop!"

I don't recall how we ended up in such a position, but he was on his back on the car seat, and I was sitting on top of him. I tried to calm him down, reassure him that I could try to drive his car and bring him to the hospital. He was oblivious to every word. I couldn't control my crying as I held his head to my chest. "Please stop. You're really scaring me, and I don't know what to do."

Soon the shaking stopped, and his breathing seemed to be under control. I sighed with relief. He was going to be all right. I was still crying when I lifted myself off him. He pulled away and sat up in the driver's seat. He seemed confused and stared blankly at me for a few moments while I blabbered on about how scared I was. "I'm so happy you're going to be all right," I told him as I searched for a Kleenex.

Without saying a word, he turned on the ignition.

I started to laugh at the sound of the running motor. "What time is it?"

He didn't answer.

I wondered why he was so angry with me. Anxiety rushed through me as familiar feelings surfaced. I didn't dare say a word for fear of delaying the drive home. He dropped me off in front of my house and drove away. I never saw him again.

Mom seemed pleased that I had obeyed her and had arrived home earlier than expected. "How was the movie?" she asked.

"The movie was great, but the man had seen it before, so he insisted we leave."

"Where did you go?"

"We parked in the bushes. His car broke down for a while and he had an epileptic fit. I was so scared. What am I supposed to do when someone has a fit like that, in case it happens again? You never know." I stared at her, hoping she would reassure me that I had done the right thing and maybe explain what to do in the future.

It didn't happen. Her expression changed to anger, and she sent me off to bed.

I shrugged my shoulders and couldn't understand why my mother was so upset with me. I went to my room and promised myself I'd never go to another movie with someone I didn't know, in case the same thing happened again.

Chapter 12
If the Shoe Fits

The early arrival of winter covered the streets with an icy snowfall that enabled us to skate to the rink half a mile from home. Ten-year-old Timmy had outgrown his skates but was desperate to join in the fun. Opportunity knocked when a neighbor offered him a pair of second-hand skates if he'd lie in court regarding a local feud. Without seeing the skates, he agreed.

"Timmy! What are you doing downstairs?" I yelled out.

He didn't answer, so I ran downstairs to see what he was doing. He had meticulously coated a pair of girl's skates with black shoeshine and was scraping the tips to make them look more like a pair of boy's skates.

On the way to the rink, we often stopped at a favorite spot at the top of a hill and waited for a bus to come by. Unaware of the danger, we grabbed onto the rear of the bus as it drove downhill and around a corner. Sometimes we lost our grip and slid under the bus, across the middle, and between the sets of front and back wheels. I don't recall ever having been afraid.

We spent hours skating hand in hand to the music of an old scratched record. We warmed up our frozen toes in a little shack that had a wood stove in the center, then headed back to the rink. We skated until the closing alarm at nine o'clock yanked us back to reality. We had escaped from the grim existence of home for a while, which made switching from one world to another somewhat easier. Back at home, we warmed up near the wood stove in the kitchen, then slipped off to bed and hoped that the rest of the night would be as peaceful as we felt.

#

My winter boots were too small, so Dad and I headed to the department store. One warm pair caught my attention, but because I didn't want Dad to spend too much, I settled for the least expensive pair. That evening, Dad pulled me aside, handed me the bill for the boots, and said I owed him the money. I didn't argue but agreed to pay him with the money I'd receive from babysitting. I was angry that I hadn't anticipated this sudden twist. Otherwise, I would have chosen a warmer, more expensive pair.

#

One Sunday, as I sat in church listening to the sermon, I found the words intimidating but I easily read between the lines. The preacher gave a sermon about how women should bear as many children as possible and not use birth control. Women should stay home and take care of their children and husbands, while the man of the house should work twelve to fourteen hours a day to provide for them.

The priest encouraged his parishioners to contribute money to the church so that he could live comfortably and abide by his priorities, which included taking a trip south each year. He made it sound as if giving money to the church was more important than feeding the children. To support his request, he recounted the story about a woman who gave away her last quarter to the church and found a dollar as she walked out the door.

At the first signs of winter each year, we went through the same ritual at Sunday mass. The priest hunched over the pulpit looking tired and pale, his hair parted in a way that made the roots of his gray hair visible. But all I saw was a man in need of a dye job. He was not well, he claimed, and had to take a vacation. The fervent parishioners, believing they were paying their way to heaven, emptied their pockets and donated their last dollars to his cause.

A week before the priest's well-deserved trip, he stood at the pulpit. Filled with a sudden burst of energy, his hair dyed pitch black, he thanked his parishioners for their generosity. At the end of his sermon, he announced that he'd be away all winter. It was difficult to understand why the parishioners didn't—or perhaps wouldn't—grasp the significance of his annual request.

I learned that parishioners could pay for masses before they died. If they paid for masses before they died, they would have free entrance to heaven. This upset me because my parents didn't have any money. I had a hard time understanding how such a proposal could be valid. Rich people could pay their way to heaven, whereas the poor didn't have a chance in hell. If this seemed logic and possible, why couldn't we accumulate prayers to be used when we had an urge to sin?

Confession was a monthly obligation at school. Children lined up in the basement hall to confess their sins. The priest sat behind a wood partition while each child knelt before him, confessed their sins, and prayed for forgiveness. What could a twelve-year-old child have to confess besides stealing carrots and praying for their Dad to die?

It was my turn. I knelt and began saying the Apostles' Creed. "Forgive me, Father, for I have sinned." Included on my list of sins was the time I ate stolen candies that my Protestant girlfriends had stolen. Before the priest gave me my penance, I wanted him to know that I hadn't really sinned because I hadn't stolen the candies. I only ate them. I was quite aware of the commandment, "Thou Shalt Not Steal."

He wasn't impressed with my reasoning and gave me a lengthy penance: I had to say the whole rosary.

I was quite upset. "Would you have given me the same penance if I had stolen the candies myself?" I asked him. I was so caught up in trying to understand why he had been so strict with me that I hadn't noticed he was fondling me. In the next instant, I looked up at him.

When his eyes met mine, he immediately moved away and made the sign of the cross.

I stood up and, with my head bowed, walked past my school friends and headed straight home. I felt sick to the stomach. Who gives the priests their penance? This priest must have to say a whole bunch of rosaries.

More questions flew through my head. Why had the priest fondled me? Did he fondle everyone? Was it normal? A priest is someone holy and pure that you should respect, isn't he? After all, you're confessing your sins to him. He must have direct contact with God, right?

By the time I arrived home, I was a wreck. I was afraid that

Mom wouldn't believe me if I told her what had happened with the priest. I became angry and started to scream at her. "Mom, I hate going to confession. I don't want to confess my stupid sins anymore."

"What did you confess?" she asked.

I told her about the stolen candies but her interest shifted to what I hadn't confessed. She asked a lot of questions, as if she wanted to make sure that my confession had nothing to do with the family.

"You're confusing me, Mom. It's not about my stupid sins anyway." I proceeded to tell her how the priest had touched me.

Her immediate reaction was to send me to my room. She warned me never to mention such accusations again. "A priest is God," she said, "and it's your fault."

I ran upstairs in a rage, screaming, "Are you saying God touched me? That's what you're saying, isn't it?"

She either didn't believe me or didn't want to. I vowed that I'd never return to confession again. However, I did go a few times afterward. I had several sins to confess, such as answering my mother back, praying that my father would die, and eating delicious stolen candies. My sins were a carbon copy of the month before. Would I ever learn?

The next time I went to confession, I was afraid I'd get the same lengthy penance. So I planned to catch the priest off guard. Before he dealt out my penance, I asked him if priests were allowed to have girlfriends.

His response was a firm. "No."

"So why are you always at the Polish woman's apartment on Main Street?" I asked. "All the kids in school are saying that she's your girlfriend."

After a brief pause, he hastily made the sign of the cross and told me to go.

I was pleased. I had received no penance this time, but I felt a bit guilty, so I said a couple of prayers and figured we were even.

Chapter 13
Sweet Sixteen

When I turned sixteen, Dad gave me a quarter to go see a movie. This was the second movie I would see and the one that would have a lasting effect on the rest of my life. I was standing at the back of the theater during the intermission when an attractive boy came up to me. He looked straight into my eyes, squeezed my arm, and smiled. "Hi, black beauty."

My knees went weak, and I almost stopped breathing. He was gorgeous! Who was he? Did he know me? I stroked my arm where he had touched me and replayed one of the most intense and exciting moments of my life. He had touched me, so why didn't it feel wrong?

I stood at the rear of the theater and scanned each row, hoping to find him. I spotted him sitting next to a girl. I stayed at the back and, when the movie was over, I saw him walking toward me.

He paused and smiled at me. "Bye, black beauty."

I didn't care that he was with another girl. I was so excited that he had taken the time to talk to me. I had never seen such a lethal combination in a young man—jet-black hair, piercing black eyes, dark skin, and full lips. I was in love!

Later I told Mom that I had seen a handsome young man who had taken my breath away. After I described him, she said she knew who he was. Her sister had gone out with an older relative of the young man. Mom told me that many women thought the men in that family were the best-looking ones in town, but they had a bad reputation for alcohol abuse.

For two weeks, I begged and pleaded with Mom to find him. It would be perfect. I could invite him to my graduation dance. To my amazement, she agreed, but on one condition: I could go to the graduation dance with him, but then I was to forget about him. She didn't want me to socialize with "that " family. I agreed to her terms, even though I was determined not to keep my promise. I had lied and deliberately broken a "thou shalt not" rule, but I didn't care.

Mom found a phone number I could call. It turned out that the young man's name was Sam, he was eighteen years old, and he was a boarder at his aunt's place. When I heard his voice, I could hardly speak. Somehow I managed to ask him to accompany me to the dance. He told me he had to work that day and couldn't make it. I hung up and felt as if my world had fallen apart.

Weeks later, my girlfriend Dina and I were walking along the beach when someone grabbed my ankle. My first reaction was to run, but I looked down instead.

It was Sam. He smiled that beautiful smile and said, "Hi, black beauty."

My heart skipped a beat. "Hi."

He invited Dina and me to stretch out on the beach blanket with him and his cousin Pete. I felt privileged as I sat down next to Sam. His cousin kept flirting with me, but Sam soon put him in his place. We talked and laughed for a while, and Sam apologized for not having called me back.

I had to look away when he stared at me. His dark piercing eyes were like Andy Garcia's. He told me he had a terrible urge to kiss me, but he had a cold sore and didn't dare.

My response was typical of a sixteen-year-old girl who had fallen in love. "I never get cold sores."

That's all Sam needed to hear. I drifted into complete ecstasy after our first kiss. It was magical and felt as if electric currents were running through my body, sparking every nerve end. It seemed to last forever.

I stood up and slowly walked away. "Wow, what a kiss! What a feeling!" I was thinking, not realizing that I hadn't said goodbye to Sam. Dina shook me out of my trance and told me that Sam wanted my phone number. Still in a daze, I whispered it to him. He repeated it to Dina to make sure he had it right.

Several months went by. Sam still hadn't called, and I wasn't going to call him. He had to make the next move.

I went to the graduation dance with a boy nicknamed Peanut. He was tall, not bad looking, and loved to dance as much as I did. Toward the end of the evening, my friends decided to go to a club and asked if I wanted to join them. Even though I was under the drinking age, I went anyway.

I was sitting in the club, sipping my soda pop, when I felt a hand on my shoulder. "Dance with me, black beauty." It was my knight in shining armor. Sam had popped in for a drink after he had finished his four-to-midnight shift at the mine.

As he led me to the dance floor, the wonderful scent of his after-shave made me light-headed. We danced a slow dance—so close that I felt as if we were floating on air. He asked me if he and his cousin Pete, along with Pete's girlfriend, could join us at our table.

"Absolutely," I answered.

Sam and I danced all night. When we weren't dancing, we were sitting at the table. I giggled every time he spoke to me. We stared at each other and amused ourselves by breaking the little plastic spoons served in drinks.

When it was time to leave, I sat in the front seat of Sam's car—an old red car that he leased from his stepfather. Pete and his girlfriend sat in the back seat. Pete kept leaning toward the front and flirting with me. Sam was getting upset, but his cousin continued massaging my shoulders and trying to kiss my neck.

Sam dropped off Pete's date first. Pete kissed her goodbye, and then sat in the front seat with his arm around my shoulders. A violent argument erupted between Sam and Pete. I was impressed; it meant that Sam was jealous.

When Sam and I were finally alone, he walked me to the front door, pulled me to him, and kissed me goodnight with those beautiful sensual lips. I was hooked. He asked me if he could call me.

Out of breath, I whispered, "Yes, you may."

I lay in my bed that night, thinking about my enchanted evening with Sam. I carved the words "I love you" in the headboard of my bed. I knew I loved him from the first moment he walked into my life.

Two months went by before Sam asked me out on a date. Other girls had tried to get a date with him but had failed. I felt so lucky. I put on my favorite white blouse, a flared skirt, buck shoes, and layers of crinolines. Sam picked me up and we went to a movie, but I had to be in by nine-thirty.

We had sat in the theater for about an hour, when Sam announced that he had already seen the movie and wanted to take me for a ride. Déjà vu, I thought. I didn't want to let go of his hand and tried to keep him in the theater a while longer.

Yet minutes later, I was hoping that everyone in town could see us as we drove up and down Main Street. We ended up at Lovers' Lane and parked in a secluded spot surrounded by tall trees. It wasn't as if needed to look for privacy, though. My curfew was nine-thirty, so we were alone long before any other couples arrived.

Romantic music blared from the car radio. Sam slowly approached me and kissed me. His kisses were so intense that I lost my breath. Then he tried to undo my blouse. I felt strange and wanted him to continue, but the Ten Commandments flashed through my mind. I pushed him away and asked him to drive me home.

He agreed without hesitation. I didn't wait for a goodnight kiss because I was still recovering from the last one. I said goodbye and entered the house, not knowing if Sam was interested in going out with me again. Over the next few months, I'd refuse any invitation to go out because I was afraid that I'd miss his call.

Sam finally called and we went out for coffee. He fixed his eyes on mine and asked, "If I were to ask you to marry me, what would you say?"

I was just sixteen, but I knew he was the one for me. "Yes!" I blurted, and then blushed with excitement when I realized that this meant he was my boyfriend.

We went out every night of the week. Hand in hand, we walked up and down Main Street or drove around town. I felt as if we were the only couple on earth.

Then things changed. Fighting and making up became a weekly routine. Sam was old enough to go to clubs and hotels and was frustrated because I wasn't. He didn't like the fact that I loved to dance. He couldn't understand that dancing washed away all the pain and fear I endured at home.

So every other week, I went to dance class with a group of girls. We looked forward to a fun evening of dancing in our flared skirts, buck shoes, and layers of crinolines. One particular dancer caught our attention from the start. He was tiny and thin, and not very attractive, but he danced the rock-and-roll and was every girl's dream of a dancing partner. He swung us in the air over his shoulders, and flung us back and forth, never missing a beat. He had first choice of any girl on the floor. If he asked a girl to dance, she'd hang on to him until the music stopped.

My dance class hadn't even finished when Sam would appear in the doorway. I thought it was cool that he wanted to pick me up after his evening shift. Since the dancers' heads were anywhere but up and colorful crinolines filled the air, it took Sam a while to find me in the dim hall. He eventually walked up to me, held my arm so tightly that it hurt, and led me out of the dance hall without saying a word. Then he drove me home in silence.

#

Soldiers from the Canadian Armed Forces were temporarily based in our town. A military exhibition was taking place in the arena, so my girlfriend Dina and I walked the grounds, giggling at the soldiers who were flirting with us.

One soldier in particular kept following us and pointing out the different displays. Dina and I felt as if we had our own tour guide. Later he asked if he could walk me home. The three of us walked together until Dina turned a corner to go home. The soldier was much older than me. I didn't think anything of it because he was in the army, so I felt safe.

We stood for a moment in front of my house. He leaned over to kiss me. He was rough, so I pushed him away. I told him I had to go inside because my father was waiting for me, and he didn't want to meet my father, that much was certain.

He begged me to give him my name and address so he could write to me. He scribbled the information on a piece of paper and kissed me on the cheek. I ran into the house, convinced that it was the last I'd hear from him.

Six months later, I rushed into the house after school and found my mother standing in the doorway waiting for me. She waved a letter in her hands. Excited at the thought I had mail but not knowing who had sent it, I ripped open the envelope and read the letter out loud. "My dearest love." I hesitated and looked at my mother.

"Continue reading," she said.

"I'm sorry I didn't write sooner," I read in a loud voice. "I can't stop thinking about you." I looked up. "Mom, are you sure this letter was meant for me? I don't have a clue who this man is."

Mom waved her hand. "Read on."

"I'll be back in your hometown in December and I'd like to meet your parents." I continued reading. My voice wavered over the words that said he wanted to marry me. When I read the part about a beautiful negligee, I panicked. "Help me, Mom. What should I do?" I handed her the letter.

She took it and silently read it, then tore it up and reassured me that I'd never hear from that man again. And I didn't.

#

Through the classroom window, I could see Sam's car parked on the street in front of the school. I couldn't wait to be with him. Because I had been denied permission to leave, I jumped out the window and ran off to meet him. This irrational decision added hundreds of lines of "I will not leave school without permission" and "I will obey my teacher" to homework that I had already neglected. My drawing skills were exchanged for lines of "I will not" that my friends in class wrote out for me.

I became accustomed to getting zeros on my French exams, but I wasn't surprised. The quicker I finished the exams, the more time I could spend with Sam. So instead of putting French accents on the words that required them, I listed each of the different accents at the top of the exam sheet and attached a note that read: "Help yourself to the accents above."

Chapter 14
Scared Stiff

One of my aunts died of cancer when she was twenty-six years old. As Dad and I walked into the funeral parlor to pay our respects, I froze at the door. I was only six years old and had never seen a dead person before. Dad realized that I was afraid, but he yanked my arm and pulled me toward the casket. I gasped. My aunt looked like a skeleton with makeup.

Dad bent over and whispered, "If you touch her, it will take away your fear." When I refused, he lifted me in his arms and forced my hand onto her cold body. I could feel my insides trembling as I cried out for him to stop, but he didn't. The experience left me with an intense fear of the dead.

When I was fourteen, I had another scary encounter. A few of my teenage girlfriends had gathered in the washroom at school and were giggling about their crushes on boys. They mentioned that a certain boy they knew owned a car and had promised every girl in the school he'd bring them for a ride.

After dark one night, it was my turn to go for a ride with three other girls. The boys decided it would be fun to scare us a bit, so they drove deep into a cemetery. They shut off the headlights, jumped out of the car, and disappeared behind the tombstones.

The girls panicked. They scrambled out of the car and raced for the gate, but I froze. As the horrid memory of my dead aunt rushed back to me, I curled up into a fetal position on the floor in the back. I broke into a cold sweat and couldn't breathe.

The boys laughed as they were returning to the car. They thought all the girls had left until they saw me on the floor. I fueled their laughter even more, and they called me names to add to their fun. When one boy realized I wasn't moving, he touched my shoulder and asked if I was all right. My screams filled the air. They left me in the back seat and drove me home as fast as they could. My experience that night only increased my fears of anything connected to the dead.

Sam's mother told stories that gave me goose bumps. In November, she was at her best when she kept us attentive with tales of the departed. Because I still had an enormous fear of the dead, her stories of water faucets that turned on by themselves and blankets that hovered over the bed disturbed me immensely.

One November evening, I sat in the kitchen of her second-story apartment for hours listening to her incredible tales. My understanding was that, if we didn't say a rosary for the departed during the month of November, they could return and scare us during the night. Because Sam knew about my fears, he whispered in my ear that, if I told him a lie, his father who had died three years earlier would pull my toes.

By the time we left his apartment, I was chilled to the bone. The freezing wind on my bare legs didn't help. Just as I put my foot on the last step, icy hands grabbed my ankle. Sam's younger brother had been waiting under the steps. The instant he clutched my leg, I took off. Sam caught up with me two blocks away. As he held me in his arms, he understood that I was genuinely frightened.

We pulled apart at the sudden screeching of a car. It was heading straight toward us. We jumped into the entrance of a furniture store and watched the car spin out of control, hit a post, and stop inches from us.

After that close call, we called it a night. I walked into my bedroom and noticed that Nanette wasn't there. We shared a bed, and I was afraid to sleep alone. I decided to say the rosary so the departed wouldn't bother me in case the tale might be true. But after I recited the first string of prayers, I drifted off to sleep in a fetal position with my toes in my hands.

Nanette cut short an overnight stay at a friend's place and returned home to find me in a deep sleep. So as not to awaken me, she tiptoed into the bedroom. I caught a peek of her shadow in the room and went into prayer frenzy. I jumped up and down on the bed and began to recite the "Hail Mary" and the "Our Father" combined. I was sure the departed had returned to haunt me because I hadn't finished my prayers.

I finally calmed down but not without a fight. Dad, Mom, and Nanette held me down as I prayed and cried, then prayed some more. Once it was over, I told them about the scary stories I had heard that night and about the car accident.

Mom stayed up with me for a while. The next day, she called Sam's mother to ask her to stop filling my head with such nonsense.

During religion class the following week, I tried to get rational answers from the priest regarding the departed. His response did nothing to ease my fears.

Chapter 15
Inevitable Truth

When I turned eighteen and still didn't have a menstrual period, Mom was concerned and sent me to the hospital for tests. They told me I had a problem with my lungs, so I allowed the doctors to listen to my breathing but only on my back. I didn't want them to lift the front of my hospital gown. For a whole week, the doctors explained why they needed to properly examine me, but I continued to lock the washroom door every time they entered my hospital room.

Frustrated with my attitude, the doctors sent me home. "Let nature take its course," they told my mother. I had no idea what they were talking about.

I was having trouble sleeping one night, so I decided to go downstairs and sit at the kitchen table. Mom walked in and asked why I wasn't in bed. I explained how I felt. The commotion woke Dad who eyed me with concern. Mom handed me a pill and told me to go back to bed.

An hour later, I had difficulty breathing and returned to the kitchen. My heart was pounding so hard that I thought it would pop out of my chest. Dad figured I was having a reaction to the sleeping pill Mom had given me. They began to argue. Swear words pierced the air and objects flew in every direction.

I returned to my room and slept in until ten o'clock the next morning. I felt so rested. I hopped down the stairs in my oversized flannelette pajamas and opened the door to the kitchen.

Mom glanced at me and pointed to the stairs. "Go back to your room and dress."

"Why should I? I always have breakfast in my pajamas."

She grabbed my arm. "Go and see Nanette."

Confused, I yanked my arm away from her and ran upstairs. While I was undressing, I discovered that I was covered in blood from my waist to my knees. I didn't understand what was going on. I thought I was dying. I screamed for help.

Nanette rushed in and handed me a serviette from a blue box. She told me to put it between my legs. Her suggestion upset me so much that I told her exactly what I thought about it. After I had showered, I ran to the basement and hid my pajamas under a pile of clothes set aside for washing.

Nanette wouldn't give up. She took me aside and calmly explained what was happening. She told me I'd experience this bleeding every month, except if I'd get pregnant.

Her words stunned me. "You're insane if you think this will happen every month. I'm not doing this. If you want to do it, go ahead, but I'm not."

The bleeding stopped a few days later. I honestly believed that it wouldn't happen again. But by the time I had my third period, it disturbed me to think that what Nanette had said was true.

#

Every night for two years, Sam and I spoke to each other on the phone for hours. We fought, broke up, made up, and broke up again. Our arguments revolved around my reluctance to take our relationship to another level. I felt uncomfortable if his hands wandered any lower than my neck and was convinced that anything more than kissing was a sin. He accused me of having had sex with others and threatened to leave me if I didn't succumb to his needs. I didn't want to fight anymore, and I didn't want to lose him. It was beginning to weigh heavily on me. Every night, I'd cry myself to sleep.

My mother was aware of the conflict between Sam and me. I figured she blamed herself for letting me get so involved. Regardless, she held back from offering me advice about sex. So after I had considered Sam's suggestion, I told him to do whatever he wanted so he could put his doubts about me to rest.

With Sam's mother and her new husband away on their honeymoon, Sam had free access to the apartment. He led me into his mother's bedroom. Holy pictures of saints hung on floral tapestry walls and seemed to be watching us. The intense look of eagerness on Sam's face increased my anxiety. He sat next to me on the bed and began to unbutton my blouse. I froze. He kept telling me that once he slept with me, it meant that he had access to my body at all times. I was terrified about giving him this freedom, but I agreed.

When he began to touch me, I felt embarrassed and started to cry. My tears angered Sam, so he tore at my clothes. I wanted to cancel our agreement and tried desperately to get away from him. I screamed and pleaded with him to stop, but I couldn't fight him off—he was too strong and determined. When I realized that I had lost the battle, a detached feeling swept over me. I became a spectator at a rape happening to someone else in slow motion.

Then it was over. Sam stood up and walked out of the room. I couldn't understand why he had been so rough and why he had hurt me. I got dressed, sat on the edge of the bed, and waited for the verdict. Was I innocent or guilty?

He poked his head into the room and angrily said, "You lied."

His reply devastated me. What's worse, I had agreed to an open contract with him. With pain added to my humiliation, I rushed to the washroom and vomited. What had just happened? What should I do? Everybody will know what I did. I dropped to my knees and made the Sign of the Cross. "Dear God, please forgive me. I didn't know, honest."

Sam didn't drive me home that night. He was too upset with me, so I walked home alone. I sat in a hot tub and scrubbed my skin until I thought it would bleed. I took a shower, then another. I couldn't get rid of the shame that oozed out of my skin.

Things began to change. Movies and sipping sodas didn't interest Sam anymore, and he stopped me from going to dance class. I hated to give up dancing. I loved to dance. I danced while I did my chores and when I walked down the street. I danced all the time.

I met Sam at his apartment every night. I sat at the table and talked about trivial things with his family when, all of a sudden, I'd hear Sam snap his finger in the hallway. I knew what that meant. I immediately stood up and met him in the washroom. He either propped me up against the door or placed me on the floor. I fought back and told him I didn't want him to do this anymore, but he put his hand over my mouth until it was over. I put my clothes back on, waited a few minutes, and told his family that I was leaving. At home, I sat in a tub of hot water and wondered why I had given in to Sam again. Going steady was not what I had expected.

I had sometimes wondered about the muffled sounds in my parents' bedroom. Why did girls get married anyway? The idea of joining a convent became more and more inviting until I heard the story of a priest who had had an affair with a nun. There really was no refuge.

Chapter 16
Revelation

I was eighteen and had a job as a bank clerk. Varicose veins appeared behind my knees and gave my co-workers a reason to tease me. As a joke, they asked me if I were pregnant and commented on the frequency of my "morning sickness."

I laughed along with them because I knew the truth. I had had lower abdominal pain for years that had caused nausea and vomiting. The doctor had said that my appendix would have to be removed one day. The shape of my body hadn't changed and I hadn't gained weight, so I knew I wasn't pregnant. The good news was that I had no more periods. It proved that my sister had been wrong after all. I was in the clear.

But something else was changing. Sam had become more aggressive during sex. At times, he would slap my face with the back of his hand and whisper the same question in my ear, over and over. "What's wrong with you?"

I couldn't answer because I didn't think anything was wrong with me. I thought I was doing everything he wanted. All I could do to calm him down was repeat, "I love you, Sam." I later learned that my failure to respond to him during sex had angered him. Then again, I had no idea that I was supposed to be enjoying it.

My stomach cramps worsened, so I went to see a doctor. "Something is wrong with my stomach," I told him. "Can you fix it?"

He began to check my stomach but stopped and took a step back. "How old are you?" he asked.

"I'm eighteen."

He frowned and sat next to me. "Here's the thing." He put his hand on my stomach, looked straight at me, and forced a smile. "You're going to have a baby." He paused. "Did you know that?"

"Can you take it away?" I asked. "I'll wait. I'll have it another time."

"Do you want me to examine you?"

"No, that's okay."

"Promise me that you'll see your family doctor because, by the feel of it, you're going to have this baby in a few months," he cautioned me.

That night, I told Sam what the doctor had said. I sat back and giggled—more from a case of nerves than from any perceived humor about my condition.

His reply was one of a scared young man who didn't have a clue about what he should do next. He stared at me as if he couldn't believe it was true. "We'll just have to wait and see. Let's not meddle with something good." And that's what we did.

Every time I had morning sickness, I told Mom it was my appendix. If I didn't think about the pregnancy, I was certain it would eventually go away. One morning at the breakfast table, a wave of nausea swept over me. I ran to the washroom adjacent to my parents' bedroom. Timmy was entering the washroom through the door leading from my parent's bedroom. I pushed him out of the way and headed for the toilet.

While I was rinsing my mouth in the sink, Timmy hurled his foot in the air and drove his cadet boot into my back. My stomach hit the sink, and I fell to the ground in pain. I was eight months pregnant and my appendix had ruptured.

I was rushed to the hospital and admitted straight to the emergency room. A tall, thin doctor pressed his hands on my right side to evaluate my situation. His eyes went wide with surprise. "Oh, my God, you're pregnant."

"Please don't tell my mother," I whispered. "It'll kill her if she finds out."

He promised.

Hospital attendants wheeled me into the operating room. The doctors gave me an epidural, then ether and a general anesthetic. When I awoke, my mother was standing next to me. She didn't mention a word about my pregnancy, which meant that the doctor had kept his promise.

When Sam heard I was in the hospital, he rushed to my side. For the first time, I saw fear and confusion in his eyes. We were two scared kids with a huge problem on our hands.

Three days after the operation, I left the hospital and walked into the house to find a familiar scene: Dad was beating Mom. In an attempt to stop the violence, I shouted, "What's going on?"

Dad turned away from Mom, grabbed me, and threw me to the floor. Mom yelled at him to be careful because I had just had an operation. Deaf to her pleading, he kicked me in the side, stomach, and head until I fainted. I went back to the emergency room. The stitches had ripped open.

"What happened to you? You just left here," the same doctor said.

"I fell," I said.

Two weeks later, I woke up in terrible pain. I hid in the closet of my bedroom and prayed that the hurt would go away. The cramps went on for three days before they subsided. In the meantime, I grew frustrated with Nanette's questions: "Did you know that you can tell when someone is pregnant by the lines in their neck?" or "Diana, have you gained weight?" I replied with harsh, unforgettable remarks that I'd later regret. The cramps returned and were more intense. I had to tell someone about my secret.

My unmarried cousin had had two babies. Her mother—a horrid woman whom I disliked immensely—had given the babies away. Because I had no one else to turn to, I went to visit my aunt. But after I had sat in her living room for a few moments, I kept staring at the floor and couldn't say a word. I decided that I had made a mistake in going there. I stood up to leave.

My aunt grabbed my arm. "What's the matter?"

I couldn't keep the secret any longer, but I was so angry that my awful aunt had to be the first to find out about it. I started to cry. "I'm pregnant."

She smiled and picked up the phone. She kept her eyes on me as she dialed. The fact that I didn't know who she was calling made me extremely nervous, but I was too afraid to ask.

Minutes later, my father arrived. Knowing how much I disliked my aunt only added to his confusion about my presence in her home. "What's going on?" he asked, chuckling nervously.

"Let's go for a ride in my truck. I have something important to tell you," my aunt said.

I sat between them. No one spoke during the fifteen-minute trip, which created heavy tension in the air. My aunt drove to another part of town and parked in front of a dumpsite. In her warped way of thinking, she probably believed the site was the most appropriate place to announce that I was pregnant. So she did.

Dad didn't move for the longest time. He glanced at me, then turned away.

My aunt repeated, "Your daughter is going to have a baby." She sat straight up in her seat, proud to be the bearer of such scandalous news. Her face reflected a holier-than-thou expression, and she nodded her head as if to say to my father, "Take that!"

Dad looked at me and asked, "When are you expecting the baby?"

"I'm not sure, Dad, but my stomach is quite sore," I replied in a timid voice. I sensed that he was angry but not with me.

He looked at my aunt. "Are you happy now?" His voice thundered with resentment.

It wasn't the reaction she had expected. "But she must pay for having had that sort of fun," she insisted.

Dad didn't answer. After my aunt had driven us back to her house, Dad and I left without saying a word to her. A block away, Dad stopped the car. "When are you due again?"

"I don't know, but it's soon."

"Don't mention anything to anyone. I'll help you."

I was relieved that he wasn't angry, yet his demeanor worried me. Was he in shock? Maybe he regretted the beating he had given me a week ago. Whatever the reason, the change in his attitude could only benefit me.

One morning, I woke up in a bad mood from having spent half the night awake. For no reason, I lashed out at my mother. She slapped me across the face. My eyes filled with tears. My pride was hurt more than anything else. I shouted that I was going to tell Dad, and I ran out of the house. Everyone thought I lost my mind. I hated my father. Why would I go to him?

By the time I arrived at Dad's workplace, I was crying

uncontrollably. I told him that I had yelled at Mom and that I was scared to have the baby. I told him I had changed my mind. I didn't want the baby anymore. I begged him to make it all go away.

He took me home and told me not to worry. I was stunned. I had never experienced a connection like this with Dad before. His composure was calm and his colors were normal. In a strange way, this unexpected reaction frightened me yet again.

Dad asked the family doctor and parish priest to come to the house to provide support while he broke the news to Mom. I was sitting alone in my room when I heard a yell from the bedroom, followed by a blend of crying and laughter. Hours went by, brandy was served, and everyone calmed down. On the way out, the priest gave me his usual chilly stare.

Mom didn't even glance at me. Her eyes were red and swollen from crying. She looked so downhearted, that I began to cry. The next morning, she continued to ignore me. I wondered if she was hurt because I had asked Dad and my aunt for help instead of her. I eventually understood that it was due to the humiliation I had brought to the family.

That same day, I went to see the doctor. He suggested that I check into the hospital to have the baby. I would give it away for adoption, and no one would ever know I had given birth. But Mom didn't want me to have the baby in our hometown. She convinced the doctor to send me away instead. The doctor called a fellow physician in a town sixty miles away and made the arrangements. All the while, I sat in silence among these adults who were planning my baby's future as if I weren't there.

Mom drove Sam and me to the hospital out of town. We sat in the back seat and held hands like two frightened children about to bear the consequences of a decision that adults had made for us. Mom dropped me off at the front door of the hospital and told me to ask for a specific doctor. I locked eyes with Sam until the car drove out of sight. I cried as I watched them leave. Neither one had hugged me or wished me luck. I felt so alone.

I spent six days in the maternity ward, which added to my anxiety as I waited for my delivery time to arrive. The expectant women in the ward endured their labor pains differently. One was a screamer and seemed mad at the world. Another woman cried and blamed her husband for her suffering. And yet another cursed everyone around and invented swear words when she grew tired of repeating the same old ones. These women unnerved me even more, but I found comfort in chewing on the ribbons of my housecoat.

On the last day of my stay, I was so hungry that I roamed the ward looking for untouched food in trays. A woman who was about to deliver offered me her complete dinner. I went to her bedside to get the tray of food and noticed that her knuckles were white from grabbing onto the bedposts during her contractions.

"Don't worry," she said. "It will soon be over."

She captivated me and I couldn't leave her side.

"This is my third baby. I can't wait to hold it in my arms." She told me she already loved her baby. She assured me that I'd have a beautiful baby and that I'd enjoy the experience of motherhood. She said that no other love was equivalent to a mother's love for her child and that I'd love it forever, no matter what the future held.

I thought this kind of love was impossible because my love for Sam exceeded anything I could possibly imagine. Yet I reflected on her words.

My turn in the delivery room arrived. The doctor made sure the nurses knew I was getting married the following month. He insisted that they address me as "Mrs."

One of the nurses hated me from the first moment she saw me. She had red hair and would taunt me, call me Mrs. with a smirk, and always begin her sentences in the same way: "I suppose you're married," or "I suppose your husband's name is Sam." She'd stare at my ring and say in a sarcastic way, "I suppose the wedding ring you're wearing is gold."

In truth, Mom had stopped at the five-and-dime store on the way to the hospital. Sam and I had bought the ring for four dollars, but it had meant the world to me.

The labor pains intensified and I curled up in bed in a fetal position. I prayed to God to stop this and let me go home. After more than twelve hours, I decided to take matters into my own hands. I got dressed, walked down the corridor, and stepped into the elevator. I had almost reached the front door when two men apprehended me. I told them that they could let me go because I decided I wasn't going to have the baby after all. When they refused,

I insisted it was my choice and I wasn't ready. They brought me to a small room and strapped me to a table, arms at my side, and put my feet in stirrups. I closed my eyes and silently began to pray but was interrupted.

"I suppose you thought you could get away with it? I suppose you think you'll keep this bastard, don't you?" The redhead from hell was sitting at the foot of the bed and held a book in her hands.

"Oh, my God! Not you! I don't want you here!" I shouted.

"You don't have a choice now, do you?"

Nothing I could say would change her attitude toward me, so I didn't speak. After a few hours, I found the straps too tight. "Could you untie me, please, so I can sit down for a moment?"

She didn't answer.

The pain was excruciating. I had to get her attention. "I have an illness that you're not aware of, and you're going to be sorry if something happens to me."

She hurried to my side. "What's wrong with you?"

I didn't answer.

"You must tell me. I'm a nurse."

I remained silent.

Out of concern, she untied the straps.

My strategy had worked. I sat up and asked if I could use the washroom. More determined than ever to go home, I rushed toward the elevator, but two interns grabbed me again before I could make my escape. This time, they took me directly to the delivery room.

The doctors observed me for several hours. Finally it was time. The baby was on its way. Although the pain was intense, I was determined not to make a sound. I was successful but only because of misplaced pride.

When I awoke, I had a cold compress on my forehead. The doctor was sitting next to me. "The delivery was difficult and several stitches were required, but everything is all right. Have you seen your eight-pound baby boy yet?"

My heart skipped a beat, and I shook uncontrollably. "I had a baby boy! Is he okay? I hope he looks like his father. Where is he? When can I hold him?" I began to cry with joy. I couldn't believe it was possible to be so happy.

"I'll be back in a few minutes," the doctor reassured me. He did return but without the baby. A sad expression filled his eyes. "There's been a mistake, but I took care of it. You can't see your baby yet, but don't worry."

"Is something wrong with my baby?" I felt the prick of a needle.

The doctor placed the empty syringe on the side table. "The baby is just fine—healthy and beautiful." Then he explained what had happened. Right after my baby's birth, the nurse from hell had sent him off to an adoption agency. Because I was an unwed mother, she had assumed that I didn't want the baby, despite the fact that I had told her I was keeping him. "I contacted the lady in charge of the adoption agency," the doctor went on, "and she said she'd keep the baby for you until you're ready to pick him up." He gave me papers to sign, confirming that I was the baby's mother and that I'd go and get him as soon as I could. The effect of the needle kicked in and I fell asleep.

Later that day, Mom and Dad came to see me. Dad's smile and excitement was genuine as he stood at the foot of the bed holding a baby blanket, a rattle, and a little nightgown. Mom came closer and whispered that sending the baby away for adoption was the right thing to do.

But I knew better.

Dad came up to me and whispered in my ear "We baptized the baby. His name is Matthew."

I repeated the name over and over. "Matthew, I love you."

Three days later, Mom sent a friend who was a taxi driver to pick me up at the hospital. She told me that I should sit up straight and proper in the taxi and say nothing about the baby. The doctor walked with me to the cab and hugged me. "Everything will be fine. Don't worry."

When I arrived home, everyone was going about their business. No one asked questions, except for Timmy who wondered what had happened to me. Mom replied that I was fine. To erase any doubts about my state of health, she gave me a pail and a cloth, and told me to get on my knees and wash the floor in the living room and sunroom, which I did. No one else asked me questions afterward, and Mom was relieved that she had finally put an end to this matter.

The next day, Dad took me into his bedroom and showed me

more blankets and toys he had hidden in the closet. He gave me the impression that he was so happy I had asked him for help. Or maybe he felt that I did love him after all. Or maybe his attitude had changed because I had shown confidence in him. Whatever the reason, I didn't care because we formed a special bond at that moment that I'd cherish forever.

Chapter 17
Promises Kept

Wedding plans were in the works. My sister Nanette was a superb seamstress and wanted to make me a gown similar to the one worn by Bridget Bardot in a movie. I refused and settled for a simple wedding dress instead. I later regretted that I hadn't given her the chance to be creative. I never had another occasion to wear a beautiful gown and feel special again.

But nothing mattered more to me than the beautiful baby boy waiting for me at the adoption agency. I imagined the moment I'd see him again. I prayed that no one would take him away and that the lady would honor the agreement she had made with the doctor.

Dad had left for a job up north and wouldn't return until after the wedding. He didn't like Sam or his alcohol-addicted family, and even though he would never have approved of my marriage to him, Dad's absence opened the door for my escape.

Mom and Nanette rushed around making arrangements for the wedding, but Sam and I had no say in any of it. I supposed it was for the better because we weren't prepared for marriage. We weren't old enough, nor did we have the faintest idea about what we were getting into. I didn't want to get married, and I was sure Sam felt the same way.

It was time to go to church. All dressed up, I gazed at myself in the mirror and began to cry. All of a sudden, I didn't want to go through with it. My sister understood and said I didn't have to get married if I didn't want to. But I knew better. Getting married was the only way I could reclaim my baby boy.

My uncle was waiting at the church entrance. His duty was to give the bride away. He walked up to me and took my arm. I pulled away in a panic because everything was happening too fast. I composed myself as best I could and began my walk down the aisle.

When I saw Sam standing at the altar and smiling at me, it melted away the fears. He touched my arm as I walked up to him and said, "Hi, black beauty. I was afraid you wouldn't show up." He left no doubts in my mind that I was doing the right thing. I was convinced I'd live happily ever after with my prince.

But a month into our marriage, Sam grew fanatical about how I spent my time. He wanted to know what I was doing while he was at work. I had to account for every moment of every day and write it down on paper so that he could inspect the list when he came back home. He searched for unaccountable minutes when I might have been unfaithful to him. I soon learned that writing things down avoided misunderstandings between us, not to mention the beatings he gave me if he detected a time lapse in my schedule.

A lack of money meant that Sam and I had to compromise, so we lived with a widower. In exchange for paying rent, I kept the old man's house clean, cooked his meals, and paid him ten dollars a month. The old man made polite conversation, but he was so sloppy that it disgusted me. His gold teeth bothered me in particular, but I couldn't understand why.

Three months passed. I was pregnant again and on my way to pick Matthew up at the agency. I was so eager that I ran up the path to ring the doorbell. Time seemed to stand still as I waited. Why was the woman taking so long to answer the door?

Finally, a tiny elderly woman appeared in the doorway. She had a worn-out look about her, but tenderness shone through and a gentle voice confirmed it. "I'm so happy you're here," she said, hugging me.

I followed her into a large room filled with thirty-two babies in individual cribs. I was trembling and didn't know if I should laugh or cry. I did both as I walked from crib to crib and examined each baby. Then I stopped in front of a crib that held a baby with dark hair. My heart was beating so hard that I could hear it in my ears. "I'm sure this one is my baby," I whispered. "He's the most beautiful baby I've ever seen. Matthew, I'm finally taking you home," I said, crying. I removed his blanket. "He's small. Why is he so small?" I asked the woman.

"He was ill, but he's going to be fine," she hastily assured me.

I took Matthew in my arms and cuddled him. Our hearts beat as one, and I couldn't get enough of his baby smell and soft skin. I lay him on the table to dress him, but I was so nervous and afraid to hurt him, that I had a hard time putting the little shirt on him. Once he was ready to go, I hugged the elderly woman and thanked her with all my heart.

While bathing Matthew that evening, I noticed a large blue bruise on his lower back. I called the doctor and he arrived thirty minutes later. After he had examined Matthew, the doctor turned to me and blurted, "Feed the child. He's hungry."

"But what about the mark on his back?" I asked.

"Feed the baby," he repeated. "My fee is fifteen dollars."

"Fifteen dollars?" Where would I get that amount of money? I glanced at Sam who responded with a blank look on his face.

Then I remembered the baby's piggy bank. I poked a knife in the slit to dig out the quarters, dimes, and nickels, but it didn't do the job fast enough. I smashed the bank on the bedroom floor and returned to the kitchen with my hands full of coins.

The doctor put the coins in his pocket. "Feed your baby" were his last words before he left. Fifteen dollars was a heavy fee to pay for that advice, but at least we knew that Matthew was okay.

Yet a doubt kept nagging at me. I went to our family doctor and asked him about the blue mark. Subsequent hospital tests indicated that Matthew was fine. I concluded that maybe the bruise had occurred when I had had my appendix taken out or as a result of the beating Dad had given me days before the baby was born.

Chapter 18
Word of Mouth

From the beginning, Sam and I had embarked on a sinking ship with no tools for our voyage except a passionate love for each other. Whenever we argued and I became upset, he blurted, "Don't get hair-iss-tickle." I laughed uncontrollably at his pronunciation of *hysterical,* no matter how intense the argument. Soon Sam was laughing along with me. We sat on the floor, face to face, legs intertwined, until our laughter faded, leaving us with smiles of contentment.

It was more than I could say about the old man's smile. His gold teeth upset me more and more. I'd wake up in the middle of the night after dreaming that my baby had been born with a stack of gold teeth. As ridiculous as those dreams were, reality proved worse. I couldn't stand the old man's voice, the way he dressed, and the slurping noise he made when he ate. Even his snoring bothered me.

Winter gave me one more reason to dislike him. The old man and Sam would stay in their beds in the morning until the house warmed up and the smell of coffee, bacon, and eggs filled the air. But even before that, I'd have to chop the wood for the stove that sat in the center of the kitchen.

But it wasn't all work and no play. The first winter that Sam and I spent together had its fun moments. After a fresh snowfall, we often rushed to the backyard and laughed as we made snow angels. The wind had taken a break, the smoke from the chimneys rose high and straight, and our "I love you's" hung frozen in the air. We hugged so tightly, it felt as if we were one. Every morning at dawn, Sam went outdoors—barefoot and in his underwear—and ran around the house several times, then rolled in the snow. When he came back indoors, I rubbed him from head to toe, and handed him a wool blanket. Sam believed that this exercise was excellent for his health. He wanted me to run with him, but I refused. I couldn't see myself running in the snow in my underwear.

Matthew was adorable. I'd sit at the foot of the bed and admire him for hours while Sam played accordion and I hummed along to the music. I never left the house if Sam was home, but when he was at work, even temperatures below zero couldn't keep me inside. I bundled Matthew up and visited my mother who lived a block away. I always called her before going over. She waited for me at the door and rushed me into the house, glancing left and right to make sure that
no one had seen me. She had everything under control. If someone happened to see me arrive or ask about the baby, I was supposed to say I was babysitting for a friend and that I was pregnant with my first child.

Mom tried to convince me that it was better for everybody's sake to stick to her story. She was afraid that I'd be the talk of the town, but I believed she was more fearful that her image might be tarnished. I listened to her unfounded excuses and saw how nervous she became every time I visited her. I felt guilty for causing her so much anguish.

One day, I bundled Matthew in a warm wool blanket and put a pillow in the sled to make sure he was comfortable. I decided to change my routine and didn't call my mother. She was surprised to see me at her door and upset that I hadn't warned her ahead of time about my arrival.

"Mom, it's all right." I said.

She tugged on my coat while her eyes scanned the street, but I pulled back. "Mom, listen to me. It's all right."

She pointed to the door and gestured for me to go inside.

I raised my voice. "Mom, I won't do this anymore." I didn't move.

She fell silent and stared at me.

"I'm going for a walk with Matthew. I'm going to show him to everyone I meet. I want everyone to know he's mine." In spite of the shocked expression on her face, I turned and walked away. I knew I had hurt her again. Only this time, I had a good reason to do it.

I strolled down the street, head up and shoulders back, smiling from ear to ear. I was ready to confront the world. I showed Matthew to strangers and made sure they knew he was mine. Then I went to the bank where I had worked. I took Matthew out of the sled, walked up to a teller's wicket, and sat the baby on the counter.

Everyone rushed over to see him. After I had answered their curious questions and confirmed that the baby was mine, I studied their reactions. I could see their little brains working overtime, trying to figure out when I had become pregnant. What a bunch of busybodies!

One girl told me she knew I had been pregnant because of the vein she had noticed behind my knee. Now that I had satisfied her curiosity, she strolled away, giggling and delighted that she had been right. Everyone agreed that I had a beautiful baby and that he looked like Sam. I already knew that, but it was nice to hear it from them anyway.

Three hours later, I walked back to my mother's house. Mom must have been looking out the window, waiting for me to return, because she called me inside before I reached the door. When I told her about my adventure with the nosy bank employees, her eyes went wide. My admission shocked her, but I was so proud at what I had accomplished that I couldn't stop laughing about it.

I continued my walks every day and met more people. By the time summer arrived, the gossip about me had dwindled away.

#

I didn't eat well during my second pregnancy, so I didn't gain much weight. I hadn't seen a doctor except for one visit at the beginning of my term. At two weeks past my delivery date, I walked into his office and pointed out the error in his calculation. "You told me I'd have my baby two weeks ago. Why hasn't it happened yet?" I also told him about the lower stomach pain that prevented me from sleeping.

The doctor frowned as he studied my slim body. "You can't possibly be pregnant. Come back in five or six months." He probably assumed I had miscarried since I hadn't returned to see him in months.

When I insisted that he examine me, he asked me to bend over and touch my toes. I did it without a problem—I had only gained about ten pounds. Maybe my tight-fitting dress threw him off because he repeated that I couldn't possibly be pregnant. Then he paused, as if he were recalling the time he had checked my appendix and discovered that I was pregnant. "All right. Go to the examining room. I'll see you shortly." After he had examined me, he said, "I want you to go to the hospital right away. I'll meet you there. I'm leaving on a trip tomorrow, and I want you to deliver your baby tonight."

That evening, the doctor induced labor, and I gave birth to another beautiful baby boy. Most important of all, he had no gold teeth and he looked just like his father. I named him Andrew. I now had two beautiful babies. How lucky could I be? God had blessed me one more time, and I wouldn't have to hide this one.

Sam was delighted to have another son. He smiled at me but couldn't take his eyes off my breasts, which had tripled in size. I made sure he understood that he'd better take a good look because he'd never see those boulders again. I felt relief when the hospital nuns poured camphor on me, but they wrapped me so tightly that I had a hard time to breathe.

Because the doctor suspected that I had a touch of phlebitis, he put my leg in a sling. He checked it every day and insisted that I inform him of the slightest swelling or discomfort. Nine days later, he removed my leg from the sling. I was so eager to leave the hospital that, when he asked if I had any pain, I fibbed and said no. He believed me and sent me home.

My mother stopped by the next day to check up on me. She noticed that I was hopping along on one leg and using my sore leg only for balance. I was wearing wool socks, so she couldn't see that my ankle was swollen. Since Mom was prone to phlebitis, she became suspicious and went back home to call the doctor.

An hour later, the doctor arrived at my door. "I'm disappointed that you lied to me about the pain in your leg. Would you mind removing your sock?"

With some reluctance, I did. The doctor crouched on the floor, lifted my foot, and examined it. He told Sam it was urgent that I return to the hospital. I spent the next eleven days there, more than enough time to regret my stupidity.

Chapter 19
Two Sides to Every Coin

As a young man, Sam was burdened with emotional luggage. His father had died in his early forties, and Sam had taken on the role of caring for the family. Increased responsibilities had left him little time to enjoy his teenage years. I sometimes wondered if an unhappy youth had contributed to his heavy drinking habit.

Sam had a generous heart and a great sense of humor, but when he drank, suspicion invaded his mind, clouded his thoughts, and left no room for the wonderful qualities that made our marriage so agreeable. I despised and feared him at times, only to wake up the next morning to a smile on his face that swept away the qualms and kept the wheels of our marriage turning.

As I soon learned, our relationship had its darkest moments whenever suspicion reared its ugly head. Sam constantly questioned me about the men I worked with. Every day, he accused me of wanting to go to bed with them. He stared straight at me, searching for a sign of lust that would give him a reason to empty his load of jealousy and rage on me.

And every time, I'd answer, "Why would I want that?" or "Why would I want another man?" I couldn't imagine allowing another man to humiliate me. I was convinced that every married couple was going through the same issues we were.

Even though Sam was extremely brutal at times, I occasionally saw the other side of his heart—genuine closeness. One evening, he walked into the apartment, a wide smile on his face. He said he had something to show me. He took me by the hand, and we walked to a nearby warehouse. "Close your eyes," he said, his voice overflowing with excitement as he led me closer to the building. "Okay, you can open your eyes now."

We couldn't see through the frost on the window, so we blew on it and made a circle big enough so that we could peek through it together. Sam turned on his flashlight and aimed it at a blue and white second-hand car. He took a deep breath and blurted out. "The car is ours. We'll be able to ride in it as soon as we pay for it—in five to six months." He grabbed me and hugged me for a long tender moment. Suddenly our eyes locked and we caught a glimpse of each other's soul. It was a moment of complete togetherness. We were so lucky. We had children, we had each other, and we would soon have a car.

Every month, even on the coldest winter day, we went to the finance company and made our payment. Then we walked by the warehouse and blew on the window to remove the frost so we could see the most beautiful car in the world. We laughed and danced, and hugged and kissed as we walked home hand in hand.

Spring arrived and the car was finally ours. Sam and I drove up and down the main street, hoping that everyone would look at us. We had stepped up a notch in the world and felt exhilarated.

After one proud year of owning the car of our dreams, Sam decided we needed a larger car. I was sad when we traded the old car for a Peugeot. It was like losing a beautiful trunk full of unforgettable memories. The Peugeot was a family station wagon with three rows of seats that could be transformed into a bed if needed. We were all set for a bigger family.

Chapter 20
On the Move

Sam was bored with his job, so he and a friend came up with the idea to move to a big city. We sold everything and ended up in Crystal Beach. We lived in a tent big enough for the seven of us: Sam and me, our two boys, and the other couple and their son.

One day, when our husbands were out looking for a job, two men who were canoeing along the lake spotted us. They called out for permission to come up and visit. We weren't too comfortable about it but figured that, as long as they kept their distance, it was okay. The men stepped out of their canoe and were heading toward us just as our husbands were driving into the camping site. I immediately told the strangers to go away. Without a word, they turned and walked back to their canoe.

Sam had seen me speak to the men. His expression flushed with anger, he asked me why I had spoken to them when I was married to him. I was that woman again—the flirt, the unfaithful wife—and I was going to be punished. I was relieved that the strangers had left because I couldn't imagine what would have happened had they stayed.

After we settled down in the tent that night, Sam whispered in my ear that I wasn't to make a sound. As usual, he bit my tongue and made it bleed. I let myself drift to another place once more. It was easier for me now—I could drift away even before it started. It frustrated Sam because, no matter what he did to me, I didn't respond. When it was over, he kept repeating that the strangers had felt sorry for me because I was skinny and unattractive, so I should eliminate any thoughts about them from my mind.

Weeks later, our husbands decided that they wanted to take us out. They had found a spot where we could go out and have fun. Our clothes were wrinkled, so I asked the owner of a nearby restaurant to lend me her iron when she had finished using it.

She looked at me in disdain and said, "I don't lend my iron to peasants."

Her response shocked me, but my immediate reaction was to laugh. When I returned to the camping site, I was still laughing and told everyone that we were considered as peasants. I waited thirty minutes and returned to the restaurant for milk. Before I left, I said to the owner, "I can see that a peasant's life is much more enjoyable than yours. I don't have to slave in the heat over an iron and unwillingly tend to campers, and I don't hate my job. The vacationers don't deserve you. Have a great day."

I had had my revenge and felt elated. I had learned years earlier that a person could be financially poor yet be extremely rich in compassion, love, and honesty, which can't be bought. I had been blessed with children—the most precious gift of all—and nothing could make me feel inferior.

By the end of summer, we had to find another place to call home. We traveled to a nearby town and found an apartment for rent. We made a deal with the owner. Instead of paying the first month's rent, we promised to paint the place, but he had to pay for the paint.

Since we had no furniture, we slept and ate on the floor. The Peugeot stayed parked in front of the house because the gas tank was empty. Then we ran out of money. What would we do for food? How would we care for the children?

The men found a job at a construction site. They worked for two days and on the third morning; they agreed that the digging job was too strenuous for them. They rolled over on the floor and fell back asleep. That same afternoon, they picked up their paychecks and bought groceries, cigarettes, and beer, of course. I was the only one who didn't smoke.

Every night as the sun went down, I'd place a blanket on the floor and the boys would curl up on it and fall asleep. The little angels never complained, even though they had no choice but to follow their parents' unrealistic dreams.

Money ran out again, and the smokers became restless. Unwilling to get another job, they found the perfect solution. So I went to the corner street, where crowds of people waited for the bus, and asked them for cigarettes. I gathered enough cigarettes to get the smokers through the weeks that followed, but we still had no food.

One evening, the other couple asked us to take care of their baby son while they went for a walk. Three hours later, they walked into the apartment, laughing and smelling of liquor. "We went to a high-class restaurant and ate a three-course meal, and had wine and other alcoholic drinks."

"How can you spend money on yourself when your baby needs food?" I shouted at them.

Our friend explained that when it came time to pay the bill, he pretended to look for his wallet, even though he had none. He told the waiter that he had lost his wallet and was truly sorry. The owner believed him and trusted he'd return to pay the bill the next day. Of course, our friend had no intention of going back.

We were hungrier now and, as usual, I was chosen to fix the problem. I went to a grocery store and asked the manager if I could charge groceries for my family. I don't know why but he agreed. I was careful to choose items that didn't need to be cooked. Later we sat in a circle on the floor of the apartment and devoured the food.

The next day, the men found jobs and worked for a week. They made enough money to pay for our trip back home, and they sent me to cash their paychecks. I was happy to have this task. I headed straight for the grocery store and paid the bill. We never did paint the apartment—we left after a month.

Chapter 21
Baby Boom

My boys were three and four years old, and I was pregnant again. Andrew resembled his father more every day. His captivating smile warmed the hearts of everyone who met him. Matthew shared his brother's dark features but not his easy smile. He was shy and quiet around people. The boys laughed and played together, but they also fought like brothers.

I was alone when my labor pains intensified. I called the dry-cleaning outlet where Sam worked, but he wasn't there, so his boss Cindy offered to drive me to the hospital.

Cindy told me that she had never been wrong in detecting the sex of a child before it was born and that mine was a girl. I was ecstatic, but moments before I was wheeled into the delivery room, she changed her mind and said it was a boy. By that time, I didn't care because I was sure it was a girl. My girlfriend had had a baby girl two weeks earlier and had promised to give me a bottle of Channel No. 5 perfume if I had a girl too. I looked forward to it.

The delivery of my third son, Charles, went extremely fast. I stared at the bottle of Channel No. 5 on my dresser in the hospital room. No girl could have replaced this beautiful baby boy, I thought, as I gazed at his dark skin, big brown eyes, and curly blond hair. But the blond hair wasn't acceptable to Sam.

Once we arrived home, Sam wouldn't even look at Charles. However, I did see him peek under the blanket and tell Charles how beautiful he was and how much he looked like his brothers, except for the hair. Warmth flowed through my heart, and I hoped that Sam would move past the blond hair. He eventually did—when Charles' locks fell and grew back dark and curly.

Ten and a half months later, Daniel was born. I walked into the hospital. When the attendant asked me the reason for my visit, I replied, "I'm going to have a baby. Now!"

Sam invited company over for dinner to celebrate my return home. I cooked a chicken and baked a cake. While we sat at the table, I had to keep my legs under Sam's. He told me it would prevent anyone else from touching me without his knowledge.

As I chewed my food, it dawned on me that we were eating meat on Good Friday—an absolute "thou shalt not" in the Catholic religion at that time. I rushed to the washroom to spit out whatever I had in my mouth and tried regurgitating without success. I felt horrible about having committed such a thoughtless, unforgivable sin. By the time I returned to the table, the others were licking their fingers clean, satisfied with the meal and unaware of my unsuccessful struggle with my conscience.

It was time for dessert. Two cakes had sat in the oven at low heat all afternoon. They had shrunk from nine inches in diameter to six and were as hard as rock. When I thought no one was looking, I threw the cakes in the garbage. Sam caught me in the act and decided to teach me a lesson, so he nailed the cakes to the wall—a reminder of the ridiculous cook he had married.

Chapter 22
Sleeping with the Enemy

We were making more money. Sam worked as a bartender, and I worked as a paymaster for hundreds of miners. I loved my job, but by the end of the day, I was mentally exhausted. Our married life was improving, and we had moments of warmth and compassion—except during sex.

But Sam found another way to humiliate me. He often forced me down on my knees next to our dog, Buddy. He grabbed my hair, yanked my head backward, and spit down my throat. He petted the dog and reminded me about how faithful dogs were to their masters.

One Sunday afternoon before Sam left for work, horrid ideas flashed through his mind. He insisted that I have sex with someone else and poked his finger into my forehead with every word he uttered to make sure I understood his orders. I loved Sam and would have done anything for him, but his continuous harassment about how frigid I had become and how I should sleep with someone else alarmed me.

The short Italian barber who cut my boys' hair used to flirt with me by putting his hand on my shoulder and staring deep into my eyes as he spoke. I found myself eager for the boys' hair to grow so that I could bring them to his barbershop.

"I like you, but you seem so unhappy," he often said to me. "If you ever need someone to talk to, I'm here."

I shelved his offer at the back of my mind as a place to visit if I ever needed to. But because I didn't like to depend on the kindness of a stranger, I decided to stop bringing the boys there for their haircuts.

Sam continued to suggest that I sleep with another man so

that I could learn to enjoy sex. He raised the topic every few days. The idea devastated me and blurred my thinking. One afternoon, I decided to confide in the barber about my situation, thinking he might be able to help me.

The barber lived in a bachelor apartment below his shop. My stomach did flip-flops as I stood at his door. I finally got the courage and knocked.

As he opened the door, the look of surprise on his face said it all. His long blue robe and messy hair confirmed my observations about how attractive I thought he was. We stood speechless for a few moments, then without saying a word, he stepped aside and gestured for me to come in. He sat on a chair and offered me a coffee. I refused and sat on the edge of the bed. A few minutes later, he got up, slowly approached me, and kissed me. "I waited so long to get this close to you."

I didn't push him away. It was clear I hadn't come here just to chat. But what did I want?

I lay down on the bed. He tried unsuccessfully to lift my sweater and skirt. When I told him I didn't want him to do that, he didn't insist. He continued to kiss me for a few minutes. I lay motionless, enjoying the kisses, when he abruptly stopped. I thought he was going to hit me, so I put my arms in front of my face. He looked surprised at my reaction, moved off me, and went to sit at the table, his eyes still fixed on mine.

Not knowing what to do or say, I walked out the door. Was that it? Was that what women were raving about? I didn't get it. Kissing gave me a feeling of satisfaction because it was a pleasant connection, and my body hadn't been violated for a change.

I walked along Main Street and, as I approached the hotel where Sam worked, I began to feel guilty about what I had done. I decided to go in and tell him what had happened.

Sam was placing cases of beer in the coolers and didn't see me come in. He looked so handsome in his white bar jacket that my heart fluttered with excitement. Two men sitting at the bar tried to make conversation with me but my eyes stayed on Sam.

Sam turned around and was shocked to see me standing there. A brief glimmer in his eyes and a beautiful smile faded as his expression changed to anger. He stared at the men at the bar then back at me. "You know this isn't a place for you, don't you?"

"I want to tell you something Sam," I blurted out.

"Go home. We'll talk later."

Back at home, I felt that I had done something terribly wrong. Yet kissing the barber hadn't seemed to be such a big deal at the time. I was so confused that I grabbed the phone and called my mother. The sound of her voice sent me into a state of agitation. The tears flowed and the guilt surfaced. "Mom, imagine the worst thing a married woman could do. Well, I just did it."

Minutes later, Mom and Dad were at my front door. I told them everything. I had calmed down and felt nothing. It was as if I were telling them a story about somebody else. They urged me not to mention a word to Sam because they knew about his jealous fits. I agreed to call them early the next day.

Sam walked into the apartment at seven o'clock in the morning. His first words were "What did you want to tell me last night?" He stared at me in a certain way, as if he were looking for evidence of a lie.

He caught me off guard, so I told him the truth. "I went to see a man. I did what you asked, but I don't feel any different."

He threw me on the bed and raped me viciously. He asked me over and over if this was what it had been like with the other man, but he kept punching me, so I couldn't reply. His rage exploded into pain as he cried out loud and held me close. He wanted me to explain in detail what had happened and I did, but I felt I had done nothing wrong.

Sam took a case of beer from the fridge and sat on the living room sofa. After he had gulped down eight beers, he decided it was time to kill the barber. "No one is allowed to touch you," he shouted.

"Sam, Sam, he's not responsible. I was the one who went to see him."

It was all in vain. He had already made up his mind.

A snowstorm had made its exit this February day, but extremely cold weather had taken its place. Without putting on his winter jacket, Sam ran through the schoolyard to take a shortcut to the barber's. But because he was drunk and confused, he walked right into deep snow and was struggling to get out.

Wearing only pajamas and socks, I rushed out the door and

plodded through knee-deep snow to reach him. He stretched his arms out toward me, and we hugged and kissed, oblivious to the cold around us. As we cried and expressed our love for each other, I wished with all my heart that I could undo the wrong and take his pain away.

Back inside, I turned on the radio. Sam and I embraced and cried as we listened to the song, "Moments to Remember," by the Four Lads. Our love was intense, but I felt as if we were swimming toward each other in a river thick with emotions, making it impossible for us to come together.

In the weeks that followed, Sam found the time to have sex with me more than once a day and asked me how I felt every time. As soon as I told him I was pregnant, he surprised me by saying he wanted nothing to do with the baby or me.

Three months later, I told my parents about my pregnancy and about Sam's attitude. When Sam was at work one evening, Mom and Dad arrived at the apartment with a bottle of wine and beaver kidneys. They were convinced that, if I drank boiled beaver kidneys in red wine, it would provoke a miscarriage. They watched me drink glass after glass of the horrible hot wine and waited for something to happen, but all I got was a major hangover and a disdain for beavers.

Four more months went by. Before Sam left to go to work one evening, he told me that a woman was coming over to abort me at eight o'clock. "Tell her you're three months' pregnant and pay her fifty dollars," he yelled and threw the money on the floor.

"There's no way I'm going to have an abortion!" I shouted back at him.

His eyes blazed in anger. "I have a message for you," he said, digging his fingers into my chest. "I want that thing gone by the time I return, and you know better than to disobey me."

At eight sharp, a plump woman with sandy blond hair tied back in a bun knocked at the door. She walked in and set her oversized suitcase on the floor. "It will cost you fifty dollars. Are you ready?"

I nodded, gave her the money, and led her to the bedroom.

After she had placed a rubber sheet over the bed, she told me to undress from the waist down and position myself on the bed. She put on a pair of rubber gloves and took out a steel rod that had a rough edge at one end. She spread my legs apart and slowly inserted the rod inside me. She poked around, but after she had tried several times and failed, she removed the rod. "Every time I think I have the right spot, the baby slips away." She frowned. "I'll try one more time." She inserted the rod and pressed very hard into my stomach, concentrating on what she could feel inside me. A wave of fear swept over her face, and she swiftly removed the steel rod. "You're not three months pregnant, are you?"

"No, I'm not," I cried. "I'm more than seven months."

"Oh, my God! I'm not touching you." She threw the fifty dollars on the floor and rushed out.

I sighed with relief and thanked God for having protected me.

The phone rang. It was Sam. He wanted to know if it was over. I didn't have time to give him all the details before the phone went dead.

I waited up for Sam that night, but he didn't come home until six the next morning. He was drunk and angry. After he had sent the older boys off to school, he took me to bed and raped me, then punched my stomach. He said he hoped he'd hurt me enough to cause a miscarriage. He was frantic and shouted that, if the woman couldn't do it, he would. "I'll punch the baby out" were his words. But he didn't succeed.

I was eight months pregnant, and I knew I'd deliver soon because the pain was so intense. When I asked Sam for his advice, he made it clear that he didn't want anything to do with the pregnancy or ever hear anything about it again.

Sam's response broke my heart. In the wee hours of a cold October night, I sat on the steps in front of the apartment building, struggling through labor pains and trying to figure out what to do next. A neighbor saw me wrapped in a flannel sheet and called my parents' home. Mom soon arrived and brought me to the hospital where they rushed me to emergency.

The obstetrician happened to be our family doctor. Mom, petite and pale, a worried look on her face, sat next to the door in the delivery room. Minutes later, the doctor held a blue, three-pound baby in his hands. I heard the snip of the umbilical cord. The doctor looked at my mother and shook his head. Mom sunk in her chair, hope slowly draining from her face. If expressions could speak, hers said to the doctor, "Please perform a miracle."

The doctor forced oxygen into the baby's lungs. She still wasn't breathing. Then he slapped the baby's bottom several times, but it remained silent and still. The doctor was about to give up when the baby uttered a loud cry, as if to say, "Hey, I'm okay. I'm here, Mom."

My mother and I sobbed.

The doctor squeezed my arm with one hand and held the baby in the other. "This baby really wanted to live. I can hardly believe it. She's tiny, but she'll be fine."

"Her name is Katherine," I said. "Katie for short."

After the hospital released me, I went back every day to see Katie in the special baby ward. She resembled a tiny porcelain doll. She had fingernails like cellophane paper, almost no eyelashes, and skin as white as milk. A fuzzy duvet covered her head. She was gorgeous, and she was my little girl.

The doctor was upset that Sam hadn't come to visit the baby or me. I tried to explain that it was my fault and told the doctor what had happened. He called Sam unmentionable names for having had doubts and insisted that this baby was none other than Sam's. If needed, he would prove it through blood work. Aware of the dire situation I was in, the doctor extended Katie's stay at the hospital. A month later, he called me. "Katie is ready to go home. She's healthy and full of life. I can't make up any more excuses about why she should stay here."

I was delighted and told Sam that I was going to get our baby.

"You're not to bring her here," he said. "She's trash and there's no room for her in this house."

When Sam came home from work the next morning, a new member of the family was sleeping on the living room sofa. His eyes glanced her way, but he made no effort to get close to her. Before he left for work that night, he stood facing me. In a slow robotic voice, as if to make sure I understood every word, he said, "I want her gone by the time I get home."

Chapter 23
Unveiled Secrets

I had to do something. Sam had disliked Katie before she was born. But without all my children, I didn't know how I'd survive. I didn't want to trigger Sam's hidden resentment toward Katie, so I worked out a plan that would appease him—at least for a while. I left the boys with a baby sitter until Sam came home from work. Then I called my mother and told her about my dilemma. She phoned my younger brother Billy who was teaching in Montreal. Dad bought a ticket and put Katie and me on a plane.

It was my first time in a plane and I was petrified. I clutched the armrests and didn't let go until after we had landed and everyone else had left the plane. I couldn't understand how people could sit back and relax while they were so high in the air. At the least, I was thankful that Katie had slept all the way through the flight.

Billy was waiting for me at the airport. A family stood by his side: a woman, her husband, and their daughter and son. They had heard of my problem and had offered to help. They told me that, if my situation worsened and if I agreed, they would immediately adopt my baby. They had already chosen the name Lynn-Marie for her. The woman took Katie in her arms and kissed her. She said she would take good care of her for as long as necessary.

I paid no attention to her remark of "as long as necessary" because my mind was miles away. I was worried about my boys and about what Sam might do when he came home and found out I had left town.

After we arrived at Billy's apartment, the landlady knocked at his door with a message. Dad had called on her apartment phone—

the only phone in the building. The landlady didn't understand what he had said because his words were slurred. Billy assumed that Dad was drunk again, so he didn't return the call. We went out for dinner and when we returned, the landlady said Dad had left another message. Billy didn't return that call either.

The next morning, Billy went to the landlady's apartment and used her phone to call home. He returned with a gloomy look on his face that chilled me.

"It's Mom, isn't it?" I asked. "Did Dad beat her again?"

He stood very still and didn't answer.

"What's wrong? Is she in the hospital? Is she dead?"

Without saying a word, Billy gently took me by the arm and led me out the door. He hailed a taxi and we rode to the bus station where we boarded a bus back to my hometown.

Half an hour into the ride, I couldn't take the suspense any longer. "Tell me what happened," I pleaded with Billy. "Is it Mom? Did he hurt her again?"

His eyes filled with tears. "A young man with no driver's license passed a school bus as the children were getting off. He hit two girls. One of them was our sister Sissy. She's dead."

I looked at Billy in disbelief. "How can that be? She's only sixteen."

From the horrified look on his face, I knew he was telling the truth, but I wasn't prepared for it. I screamed, pounded on his chest, and called him a liar. I wanted to hear another reply that was less devastating, but he had none. Our pretty Sissy, who could put lumberjacks to shame with her loud rumbling laugh, was gone.

#

My mind went back to a conversation I had had with Sissy two weeks before she died. She told me I was lucky to have children and a gorgeous husband. She loved children and had been hired as a baby sitter for all the little ones on our street. "But I'll never have children," she said. "It's not meant to be."

Sadness echoed in her voice. I wanted to cheer her up, so I told her that dreams were for everyone and that she could have anything she wanted in life. "Sissy, one day you'll get married and have beautiful children of your own."

Sissy smiled and shook her head. "No."

Her expression was so gloomy that I wondered if she knew something I didn't. Why was she so unhappy?

As if she had read my mind, she had gone on to say how much she hated Dad and that, if she lived to be eighteen, she'd put him in jail for the rest of his life. "If he dies before me, I won't go to his funeral." She paused, as if she were pondering an important decision. "I'm sure I'll die before him, but I'll make sure he never forgets me."

Before I could answer, Sissy changed the subject and showed me a pile of presents she had stashed away in her closet for the children she baby-sat. She made me promise that they would get them. I found it odd that she would say such a thing, but she was so adamant that I went along with it. Then she tried on a black dress and modeled it for Mom and me so we could tell her how she looked.

The day before Sissy died, she spent the day cleaning her bedroom and meticulously placing her clothes in the drawers. "Mom, would you come upstairs for a moment? I have something to show you." Mom walked into her room and was amazed. The usual mess that her teenage daughter had encouraged over the years was nowhere to be seen. Sissy opened the bottom drawer and made Mom promise to give everything in it to me and no one else. Mom heard Sissy's request but didn't pay much attention to it. It was as if Sissy, loud and clear, had revealed a secret to deaf ears.

Hours before I took the plane to Montreal that cold November morning, Sissy had asked me to do her hair up in baubles. I couldn't do it, so she did it on her own. When she left for school, Mom told her that she didn't like her hairdo. Sissy walked out, but when she reached the street corner, she turned around and came back home. "Do you love me anyway, Mom?" she asked and then ran off to catch the school bus. That was the last time Mom saw her baby girl alive.

#

Billy choked back the tears and told me what Dad had said during their phone conversation earlier. It seemed that the car had hit Sissy in front of the school where Mom worked, but Mom had already left for the day. Dad was on his way home and had never stopped to check out an accident before, but a nagging feeling urged him to do so this time.

The priest's residence was located across the street from the school. Dad stopped his car and heard a priest call out to him. "I think it's your daughter."

"It's impossible," Dad replied. "I only have one young daughter and she must be home by now." But as he approached the accident scene, he saw Sissy's broken body sprawled out on the ground. Blood was flowing from her nose and mouth. As Dad took a closer look to make sure he wasn't imagining it, Sissy's eyes locked on his. That moment would stay in his mind the rest of his life—just as she had promised.

Because Dad had cradled Sissy before the ambulance took her to the hospital, his clothes were stained with her blood. As he walked through the door, Mom thought he had hurt himself, but then he said, "She's dead. Sissy is dead." A horrific scream filled the air and Mom fainted.

Someone had to identify Sissy's body. The hospital couldn't reach anyone in the family except Timmy, and although he wished he didn't have to do it, he had no choice but to take on the gruesome task. He often commented afterward how the whiteness of her skin had given Sissy an unrealistic appearance, like a wax figure, and how that image still unnerved him. He had no idea how much the black dress had meant to Sissy, yet he chose it as her final resting attire.

#

It was hard to believe that so much had happened in the last twenty-four hours. As I stepped off the bus in my hometown, Sam greeted me. I looked into those beautiful eyes filled with mixed emotions. He put his arms around me and, without a word I followed him home. I was thrilled to see my boys. One day away from them had seemed like a year.

The next day, family and friends gathered at the funeral parlor to say a last goodbye to Sissy. I approached my sister's coffin with no hesitation. The pain of loss had replaced my fear of the dead. I gazed down at Sissy, silent tears rolling down my cheeks. Her black dress made her fair complexion look even paler, but she looked peaceful, as if she were about to wake up from a nap at any moment.

I turned around and looked for Mom. She was sitting in a chair not far from the coffin, in a world of her own, oblivious to the visitors who had come by to show their respects. After she had fainted at home, Mom had spent a day in the hospital and had been released hours before Sissy's funeral. The tranquillizers the doctor had given her could have explained her passive state because Mom didn't even shed a tear during the three-day wake for her daughter. As for Dad, he was in a perpetual sate of shock.

My children were with me. Matthew and Andrew were all dressed up in brown coats with Persian lamb fur collars and fur hats—a gift from my mother. They walked around like two little gentlemen, not realizing the solemn reason behind the get-together. Katie, who was now almost two months, had lost her godmother.

I sat listening to the nuns praying in a monotone voice as they knelt in front of the coffin. I glanced sideways to where Timmy was sitting. A grin melted his weary expression, and I knew that he had noticed the same droning sound. We started to laugh. We were now doubled over and the laughter rapidly turned into hysteria. What were we doing? How could we laugh at such a tragic time?

The next day, we sat apart in case we'd laugh again. Everything went fine until I looked at him. We burst out laughing. I was cold, I was sad, I was crying, but I was laughing too. After our laughing frenzy had died down, the pain of reality became intense.

Sissy was dead. How I'd miss her laughter! My little sister had always been shy around boys and men. But she liked Sam and would never refuse a hug from him now and then, even though she blushed every time. She'd never talk about what was hurting her so much, but I eventually found out.

A few days after the funeral, Billy and I were sitting at the kitchen table at our parents' home. Dad was sobbing on the sofa nearby. Mom was walking around like a zombie, anguish carved into her face. Billy looked at me, and I knew exactly what he was thinking. I nodded yes.

Now twenty-one years old, Billy stood up, glanced at Dad with contempt, and told Mom he had something to say to her. Then he revealed the dark secret we had kept hidden for so long.

One night thirteen years earlier, I had gone to Sissy's bedroom but she wasn't there. Dad was in the basement, so I asked Billy to go with me. We crept downstairs like mice and hid behind the old washing machine. I could hear Dad whisper, but I couldn't see who he was speaking to. Then I saw him lift Sissy up and stand her on a wood stump. I couldn't see what he was doing to her, but I knew it was wrong. Sissy seemed scared and confused as she stared at Dad. She looked as if she wanted to cry out but was too afraid to do so.

Billy and I edged a little closer. Frightened by what we witnessed, we tiptoed back upstairs. As we sat at the top of the stairs, a torrent of mixed emotions raced through me. Billy took my hand and, with tear-filled eyes, he whispered, "He saw me, I know he did, but he didn't see you." As if we were thinking with the same mind, we ran downstairs, across the kitchen, and down the basement stairs.

Dad stopped us. He had Sissy in his arms. He scowled at me and asked me what I was doing.

"We're playing hide-and-seek," I said. "What are you doing with her?" His stare was intimidating, but I persisted. "Is she all right?"

Those penetrating blue eyes said everything.

Billy and I slowly turned around and went to our rooms. After Dad put Sissy to bed, I went to her bedside and covered her with blankets. I hummed a lullaby, but she lay there motionless with no expression on her face as tears ran down her cheeks.

Billy's voice choked up before he could finish, so I jumped into the conversation. I revealed everything we saw that night and many other nights that followed. The pain in telling Mom about our secret was worse that I could have imagined. Billy was crying, but he had had the courage to turn toward Dad as if to challenge him to deny it. I was crying so hard that I couldn't quite make out Dad's expression, but I figured it wasn't a happy one. My brother and I had dared to go against him, and he couldn't defend himself.

"Dad!" Billy said. "Diane saw you too. She was with me and she never revealed our secret despite your beatings. Maybe that's the reason why I never got a beating. Right, Dad?"

"And Dad," I added, "even though you didn't beat Billy and you gave him everything he wanted, you destroyed him like you've destroyed everyone else."

Billy sat with his face in his hands and sobbed. "I'm sorry, Mom, for not having told you earlier. I'm so sorry." He looked up at me and took a deep breath. "It's finally out. We're going to make it. I'm sorry for the beatings you and Timmy went through. You didn't deserve it."

I was relieved that Billy had freed himself of the heavy burden of secrecy. The physical abuse the rest of us had endured was nothing compared to the mental torture he had suffered. He had been Mom's pet and, consequently, Dad had never laid a hand on him. As we were growing up, Timmy and I had envied Billy, but we had been wrong all along. There was nothing to envy.

Billy and I turned our attention to Mom who hadn't said a word so far. She stood in the middle of the floor, tiny and pale, drained of all emotions. Her eyes had glazed over, like one who had experienced a terrible shock and couldn't absorb any more. No surgeon could ever remove the wrinkles of grief embedded in her fair complexion. She had lost her baby and had finally discovered why Sissy had hated Dad so much. We reached Mom's side too late and watched as she collapsed to the floor.

Chapter 24
Disowned

As horrid incidents with Dad and Granddad flashed through my mind, I recalled the Bible passage that referred to sins passed down from the father upon his sons. I was certain that bad blood had been transferred from my great-grandfather to my grandfather and to my father. It was the only logic that could explain the suffering that one generation seemed to pass on to the next.

Regardless, I sensed a definite change for the better. Bad blood might have disrupted our lives to a degree, but I was optimistic that it would dissipate with the unfolding of my children's future.

Sissy's funeral was over. I was sitting at the kitchen table remembering her loud laugh, when I felt Sam's eyes on me. Had he forgotten about Katie? How had he reacted when he had found out I had left town?

"Where did you leave her?" Sam's face showed no emotion.

"In Montreal. A couple is taking care of her."

"You can bring her home," he said, squeezing my hand in his.

My heart filled with joy, and I thanked Sam over and over. I grabbed the phone to call Billy. A familiar fear of losing my baby resurfaced, and I hoped the woman remembered that she only had Katie temporarily.

My worries were put to rest when Billy hopped on the next bus and brought Katie home. My little porcelain doll was in my arms at last. Her beauty astonished me, and I held her for the longest time. I placed her on the couch while I stepped into the washroom.

As I was heading back toward the living room, I saw Sam lift the blanket and peek at Katie's face. It was the first time he had seen her. He was talking out loud, telling her how pretty she was and how much she looked like Charlie. She had blond hair, he said, but she had blue eyes like her mother. The notion that Sam had reached out to Katie in this way made me so happy.

He heard me approach and immediately covered Katie's face. He told me to sit down because he had something important to say. "She's not ours. Do you understand? No one is to know you had another baby." He grabbed my arm tightly. "You will say she's a baby we're keeping for friends. Do you understand me? I will never spend a penny on her, nor will I buy food for her. I don't ever want to hear her cry."

This can't be real, I thought. This can't be happening again.

"If someone comes over," he went on, "I want you to hide her. You'll be sorry if you don't."

Sam went about his business as if we were a happily married couple with four boys. But every knock at the door sent me scurrying to the basement with Katie. I'd gently cover her mouth with kisses or with my hand, or put her mouth on my cheek. Visitors stayed for hours while I sat in the basement rocking her in my arms. I wondered if Katie could feel my fear and kept quiet because of it. God, I believed she did because not once did I have to press my hand in the slightest over her mouth.

In December, after a month of hiding Katie, I decided it had to stop. "Sam, I'm tired of pretending. I want to tell everyone the truth about Katie."

In the middle of the night, Sam woke me up from a deep sleep. Speaking in a hushed voice so as not to awaken the boys, he asked me to put on my coat, bundle Katie up, and go with him. He had a surprise for me. I didn't know what to expect, but I wrapped a large blanket around Katie and rode off with Sam.

He drove for a while, then parked the car but kept the headlights on. I looked around. We were at the dump again! Why did everyone think this was a good place to talk? I instinctively held Katie closer. "What are we doing here?"

He didn't answer but just kept staring ahead at the pile of debris. A few minutes went by before he spoke. "Take her and put her under the garbage."

"What are you saying?" I asked, clutching Katie tighter.

"Do it. No one will ever know." His voice was calm.

I had a sinking feeling. "What's going on, Sam?"

The hatred in his eyes told me he was serious. I cuddled Katie inside my coat, slowly reached for the handle, and opened the car door. I felt weak and dizzy. The next thing I knew, I regained consciousness in the car without Katie in my arms. "Where is she?" I screamed, terrified. "Where is Katie?"

Sam had placed her on the back seat. I picked her up and began to thank him but stopped. What was I thanking him for? He laughed and was amused that he had scared me to the point of fainting. The whole time, Katie hadn't made a sound. Angels were with us that night.

I was determined that the daily trips to the basement had to stop. Sam's arguing wouldn't change my mind. I admitted to having five children, and Sam, to four. Months passed and public curiosity faded. Life returned to normal—that is, as normal as possible.

Sam hadn't shown Katie any sign of affection so far, but every chance she had, she ran up to him and tried to crawl onto his lap or hug his legs. When he pushed her away, she looked at him with innocent eyes, not knowing if she should cry or smile. Yet rejection didn't stop her. Every time Sam walked into the house, her eyes lit up and she ran to him, only to suffer rejection again.

One evening, a friend and I were looking at photos while our husbands were getting drunk in the kitchen. She seemed confused as she looked at a picture of me when I was three years old. Seeing as she didn't know that Katie was mine, she was convinced it was a picture of the little girl I was babysitting.

I took the picture from her. "This is a photo of me."

"How can that be? It looks exactly like the little girl you're babysitting."

Delighted about the resemblance, I laughed. "Well, the baby girl is really my daughter." I felt Sam's eyes on me. I knew he had heard me but I ignored him.

My friend's curiosity had been awakened and she wanted details about the secret I had kept for so long. Her husband was too drunk to grasp that Sam was trying very hard to convince him that the baby wasn't ours. At the end of the evening, my friend left with gossip that she was no doubt eager to spread.

I had just shut the door when Sam's hand struck my head. I went into a spin and my neck snapped with the force of the blow. I stared at him and pretended that it didn't hurt. The second one came across harder than the first. My ears were ringing, yet I uttered no sound as the tears rolled down my cheeks.

"Don't you ever humiliate me like that again, understand?" Sam shouted.

Chapter 25
Behind Closed Doors

The women on my street loved to come over for coffee and a flirting session with Sam. They enjoyed the attention he gave them, and they giggled and squirmed in their chairs when he spoke to them. One woman even made sure to tell Sam that her husband worked out of town and came home only on weekends.

"Call me if you get too wild," Sam would reply.

I'd listen to them and think, "What in the world is going on? If she wants to have sex, she must be sick." It never dawned on me that I was the one who had a problem.

Because of my lack of interest in sex, Sam's mind sometimes went into overdrive. One night, he entered the bedroom with a large bottle of beer and wanted to put it inside me. "Prostitutes sit on them, so you can too."

The eagerness in his eyes petrified me. My unwavering reluctance to participate in his insane suggestions angered him, but I never gave in.

Sam once planned a surprise for me while we were having sex. He lit two packs of matches at once and burnt my pubic hair and skin. I screamed in pain, but Sam paid no attention. He decided that having more sex was the next appropriate thing to do. "I don't know why I even bother with you," he shouted at me afterward. His perfect explanation was that, if the fire hadn't burned me, it would have meant that I had caught a disease.

In the evening while Sam was sleeping, I was restless and went for walks. It was dark and cold the first time I entered the cemetery, but I wasn't afraid. I ended up sitting with my legs crossed on the grass over Sissy's grave. I told her how much I missed her and related everything that had happened since she left. I talked about my children and disclosed secrets, knowing she wouldn't tell anyone. I told her I hoped she was happier now than when she had been on earth. "Sissy, sometimes I wish I were with you." I stood up to leave, then turned around and whispered, "I miss you so much, Sissy, but I'm glad you're free."

Talking to Sissy lessened my burden somewhat, but I needed to get professional advice about my relationship with Sam. I decided to see the family doctor. I told him how I hated it when Sam touched me and how I hated the roughness of sex. I pointed out that sometimes Sam wanted to have sex three times a day. I related how painful and disgusting sexual intercourse had become, and how I wished I could stop it. I admitted that I put my hair in rollers and walked around in slippers and a bathrobe to discourage Sam, but it didn't stop him. "I can't understand why any woman would want to have sex."

Until now, the doctor had leaned back in his chair and appeared to be intrigued by what I was saying. "Did you know that women enjoy sex?" he asked me. "It's a wonderful experience."

That was all I needed to hear. I sprung up from my chair, convinced that I had made a mistake by telling a man about my dilemma. I waved my arms in the air and said, "You're a very sick man, did you know that?" I paused. "You're a pig. Why did I think you were any different? What the hell is wrong with you men anyway?"

As I stormed out of his office, he called out to me, "I'm sorry. Come back."

"You're sick!" I yelled at the top of my voice, not caring who heard me.

Later I thought about it. Maybe I was wrong. Maybe I should at least try harder to enjoy sex. When Sam came home, I showed him my list of activities for the day. He had dinner and fell asleep, and when he woke up, he was ready to have sex. I tried, but his aggressive behavior revolted me. I vomited in bed and it made the situation worse. I tried to tell Sam that I was truly sorry and that I didn't know what was wrong with me, but he didn't listen.

The next day, he brought his friend Steve home. After they

had become drunk and silly, Sam grabbed me and started to dance around the living room. I was laughing and having fun, and didn't notice that Sam had pulled up my dress, giving full view of my backside to Steve. When I grasped what was going on, I ran into the washroom and locked the door, but Sam came charging in. He dragged me back to the living room and wanted to dance again.

Steve suddenly stood up, told me he was terribly sorry, and left. Sam called out after him, said there was a misunderstanding, and that everything would be all right. But Steve didn't come back.

Upset at the outcome of the evening, Sam shoved me against the wall and slapped my face a few times. He proceeded with the usual violent and painful rape. When it was over, I vomited over and over until I couldn't anymore.

"You make me sick. I don't know why I stay with you," Sam said. "Nobody cares for you. You'd be better off dead."

I went to the washroom and took a long hot shower. I scrubbed my body until my skin hurt. Standing naked in front of the mirror, I stared at my reflection. I was skinny, pale, and ugly. In other words, horrendous. How could I think I was deserving of Sam's love? He was right: I'd be better off dead.

I spotted a razor blade on the sink. I picked it up and slashed my left wrist. I was going for the right one when Billy arrived home for the weekend. He must have sensed that something was wrong because he headed straight for the washroom and stopped me just in time. The blood was squirting directly from my wrist to the wall with every beat of my heart.

"What's wrong with you, Sam?" Billy said. "Can't you see that Diane would die for you?" He wrapped my wrist and brought me to the hospital.

"Why are you two still together when all you do is hurt each other?" Billy asked me later when we were alone.

"I love him," I replied, "but if he'd be happier without me, I'd have no problem leaving him. I'm not afraid to die."

Months later, I received a letter in the mail—my second one ever. It was from Steve. "Why would he write me a letter?" I asked Sam.

In the letter, Steve apologized for having been drunk when he came to our home and for having caused trouble. He went on to say that he was in love with me.

I gasped. I had had a similar experience before, and I didn't like it. "Why did he write a silly thing like this, Sam?" I handed him the letter.

Sam read it out loud and grew more upset with every word. Once he had finished, he decided that I had to be punished for having provoked such feelings in his friend. Never understanding what I had done, I paid the price and again made blank promises. I never saw Steve again, and he'd never know the pain his letter had caused.

Chapter 26
Boys will be Boys

Nanette sent me a package that contained Christmas gifts she had made: four red flannel pajamas for the boys and a red nightgown for Katie. The children were sitting side by side on the sofa, admiring their gifts, when my friend Sally called. She needed to talk to me in private. My usual baby sitter wasn't available, so Sally sent over her twenty-three-year-old brother. He seemed a bit worried when he saw the couch stacked with children.

"Will you be all right?" I asked him.

"Sure, I have a brother. I'm used to babysitting," he answered.

I wasn't convinced, so I asked him to call me at Sally's if he had any problems.

During the next two hours, Sally confided that her jealousy had triggered arguments with her husband. "I wish I wouldn't do that to him. I don't know what's wrong with me."

"Sally, you must calm down," I told her. "You know you have a great husband. Your silly accusations will drive him away."

I was sad to see the similarities in our lives but offered advice that I hoped would help her. Once she understood that her accusations could harm her marriage and she could actually lose her husband, she burst into tears. She thanked me and said she'd try my suggestions.

As I walked up the laneway to my home, I could hear the children's screams and laughter. I opened the door and found the baby sitter spread out on the floor, his hands and feet tied to the sofa legs. He had agreed to play cowboys and Indians with my boys but couldn't imagine the seriousness of four Indians attacking a single cowboy. His frustration and humiliation was obvious, and for an instant, I was glad he was tied.

#

One afternoon I took the children to a department store. Keeping the boys in sight every moment was impossible. As they eyed all the beautiful things, it reminded me how much I had admired such unattainable treasures in my younger days. Counters of colorful bulk candies in transparent bins proved too tempting for Matthew and Andrew. They pulled out of my grip and darted straight for the bins. They stuffed as many candies as possible in their mouths and pockets before anyone noticed what they were doing.

The clerk, who was too overwhelmed to speak, stood staring as the children gobbled up jelly beans in record numbers.

I spewed out several apologies and hastily walked out the store while scolding the boys. I knew they had broken the "thou-shalt-not-steal" rule, but deep inside, I was happy they had obtained a treat.

#

My son Charlie had been quiet for the past few days. Something was bothering him.

"What do you have in your coat pocket, Charlie?" I asked.

His eyes reflected sorrow mixed with love and confusion. "A dead bird. If I hold onto it, it will come back to life."

I suggested that we bury it. He reluctantly agreed but wished he had another choice. We carefully placed the bird in a matchbox, dug a hole, and made a cross with twigs to put on the gravesite.

Hours later, Charlie was pacing the yard again with his hand in his pocket. I noticed the hole had been dug up and the matchbox was empty. He assured me that the bird was better off in his pocket, and I agreed.

The next day, a taxi arrived to take my children and me into town. We were going shopping.

"Charlie," I said, "it might be best if you leave your coat and the bird in the washroom. You can take care of it when you get back."

He agreed, but I deliberately left my purse on the table and used it as a reason to go back inside. I wrapped the bird in paper, put it in the garbage can, and opened the bathroom window.

When we returned from our shopping trip, Charlie headed straight for the washroom. He was shocked to see that the bird was gone and questioned its whereabouts.

I pretended to be surprised and pointed to the open window. "Maybe your bird flew away, Charlie."

A look of doubt lingered on his face, but then he smiled as if he hoped it were true.

While I was hanging the laundry outside, I saw Charlie waving to a bird perched on a telephone line. "I knew you weren't dead. I'm so happy you're okay, little bird. Look Mom, my bird's on the telephone line."

That same night, a buzzing sound prevented me from falling asleep. I searched the bedroom and found a jar of bumblebees hidden under my bed. They were Charlie's pets.

#

Years later, our family moved to the country. One afternoon, a child's laughter outside distracted me from my cooking. Charlie was sitting on the neighbor's pony and was heading straight toward the house. The pony stopped abruptly and threw Charlie in the air. He landed on his bottom in deep snow and, in the next second, his wool cap landed on his head. The wide-eyed expression on his face in that picture-perfect moment was priceless and still brings a smile to my face.

#

The children and I often spoke of things that we wanted to do.

"Mom, when I grow up, I'm going to buy you a blue dress, blue shoes, and a blue purse," Charlie promised as I cleaned the house.

Andrew heard the declaration and wanted to top it. "Mom, when I grow up, I'm going to buy you a pink dress, pink shoes, a pink purse, *and* a pink necklace."

Seconds later, another young voice from the washroom made the same promise but changed the color of the items and added a bracelet.

I usually finished most of my housework by mid-afternoon and took the occasional nap before Sam came back from work. I'd flop down on the bed, and one by one, the children would make their way to me. I loved the touch of their little hands in my hair as they made knots and ponytails. By the time they were done, I'd be sound asleep.

Even Sam supplied the children with a playground of sorts. After he fell asleep, I'd shave his hairy legs to create "roads" for the boys to play on with their matchbox cars. They drove the cars up and down his legs, causing accidents that didn't bother the motionless participant.

I sat by the children's bedside at night and watched them sleep. I felt so blessed to experience the gift of unconditional love. "Please God," I prayed. "I can face any challenge, but please don't ever take any of my children away from me because I'd surely die."

Communication between the children and me never stopped. We even talked in our sleep. Andrew and I had conversations during the night without waking or leaving our beds. He called out from his room, and I immediately answered. Our conversations seemed to make sense as we chatted through the night.

One night, Charlie whispered in my ear, "I'm hungry, Mom."

"You can have the hamburger in the fridge," I told him.

When he went to the fridge and couldn't find it, he came back to my bedroom and whispered, "Where is it, Mom?" He put his ear over my mouth to hear what I'd say.

"It's in my top drawer."

He hesitated but looked in the drawer anyway. His stomach gurgling as he moved things around in the drawer.

I was talking out loud again, so Charlie put his ear to my mouth and waited for a clue. "Water the rose that's in my drawer, please," I said before I drifted into a deep sleep.

I apologized the next morning after Charlie told me what had happened. He was frustrated because he had been eager to get his teeth into the hamburger. He thought that he might miss out on a good meal if he didn't find it before one of his brothers did, but he finally understood there was no hamburger and that a peanut butter sandwich would have to do.

A lesson learned. Never believe anything that Mom says unless she's sitting up wide-awake in front of you.

#

Sam and I always owned pets, but the German shepherd was our first choice.

I was walking to my parents' house with Lucky, our five-month-old female German shepherd, when a female adult German shepherd attacked her. The adult dog had broken away from her leash in a neighbor's back yard.

I had no time to react. She bit into Lucky's hip and crippled her instantly. I pretended to lunge at her to scare her off, but she bit Lucky in the stomach and tore off a piece of her fur and flesh. Lucky lay helpless on the ground. The other dog had killed her own pups at birth, and I knew nothing would stop her from killing Lucky.

All of a sudden, a neighbor arrived and hit the other dog over the head with a floor ashtray. The dog fell to the ground, giving me just enough time to pick Lucky up and run back home.

As I was shutting the door behind me, the neighbor's dog leapt up against it. She was foaming at the mouth, and only a thin sheet of glass separated us. The neighbor scampered up to her, put a collar on her, and led her away.

I had heard about a healer and brought Lucky to him. I figured that, even though Lucky was a dog, she was worthy of human healing. The healer took the dog and placed her on the table. He gently touched every limb in her body. Without a whimper from Lucky, all dislocated joints were put back in their proper place. Broken bones were strapped up and a dressing was placed on her stomach.

We tended to Lucky's wounds for weeks. When her stomach healed, her therapy began. She ran around and became one of the best dogs we ever had. She played with the children but kept a vigilant eye out for intruders.

#

I was excited about a weekend trip, but I began to miss the children even before we left. Two days later, we returned to a home filled with endless crying. The boys had lost their pet. They had petted Lucky goodbye before going to school that Friday. After she had watched the children go off, Lucky had gnawed at the rope that kept her within our property limits. By the time the boys arrived in the schoolyard, she was waiting for them.

A teacher wanted to know who owned the dog, and the boys were happy to say that she was theirs. The teacher ordered them to send her home, but Lucky wanted to stay. The teacher approached the dog and kicked her. Lucky became upset and snapped at the teacher's leg. Blood trickled from a leg that was already covered in varicose veins, making the situation look worse than what it actually was. The police were called, and Lucky was taken away. It was the last time the boys saw their dog.

The children were devastated, and Sam and I shared their pain. Lucky had been a perfect pet. Months later, we bought another three-year-old German shepherd.

#

One afternoon, I walked into my parents' house and caught my father with his fist in the air. He was about to hit my seven-year-old son Andrew for a silly reason. While they had been roughing it up on the floor like a couple of kids, Andrew had accidentally hit my father's nose with his knee, and it had infuriated Dad.

When I saw that Dad was about to lose control, I pushed him to the ground and stood over him. "You are never to touch any of my children," I yelled. "Do you understand?" I paused. The message had to be crystal clear. "You spent your whole life destroying everyone in your path. But now, your reign has come to an end. If you ever touch any of my children, I'll have no choice but to kill you. And I will."

Dad wiped a drop of blood from his nose. "No one ever made me bleed, and it certainly won't be a kid of yours," he grunted.

I left the house, relieved that I had arrived in time. I promised myself that my children would never experience the consequences of my father's anger. Had I walked in seconds later, I might have lost control. I couldn't imagine what I would have done.

#

It was April fool's day. Who could I play a trick on? I glanced out the kitchen window and saw Dad drive up to his house. I decided he'd be the one. He had a half hour for lunch, so I waited ten minutes before I called him.

I made my voice sound frantic. "Dad, you have to come over right away. Someone broke into your shed, and they're stealing all your tools."

There was no response.

I giggled as I watched him jump into his red Chevy, back out of his driveway, and turn the corner on two wheels. He arrived at my front door in a huff. His face was pale and his ears were red. He reminded me of Bugs Bunny.

"Where are they?" he asked.

I looked out toward the shed he had built to store his tools. "Oh, they've already gone. I was sure I saw two fish stealing your tools."

"Two what?" he shouted.

"Fish." I spelled out the word to make sure he understood.

Dad wasn't used to jokes, so it took him a few moments to understand what was going on. His face turned blood red and his eyes, dark blue. I had seen that look before but no longer feared it. Well, maybe a little. He pointed a finger at me and said, "Damn you! I don't ever want to see you again. Damn you!" He drove off, spinning gravel and dust in the air.

Two weeks later, Mom was still warning me to stay away. But I believed that Dad's behavior was childish, so I marched over to their house. I was nervous when I opened the door. Dad was having lunch. His face flushed as he looked up at me.

"Dad, may I come in? Are you still upset?" I tried to keep my voice calm. He didn't answer, so I took a chance and sat at the table facing him. He stared at me, but something about him was different. His eyes reflected a trait I had never seen in them before: amusement. So I did what came naturally: I laughed out loud.

"Are you still angry?" he asked me.

"Angry? I was never angry. What about you, Dad?" I could see that he wanted to laugh but didn't know how. I had glimpsed humor in his eyes after I had disrobed the first layer of anger, and he knew it.

"Just shut up" was his reply. Neither of us ever mentioned the incident again.

The next day, workers from the phone company came to my door to ask if I had a sledgehammer. I didn't have one, so I ran to Dad's house to borrow his.

Dad wasn't impressed with the workers. He kept yelling about how lazy they were for having sent a woman in their place. "Those S.O.B.'s sit on their asses and are paid to do nothing," he raged. "They should have come to ask for my sledgehammer themselves."

I tried to explain that it was my idea and not theirs, but Dad was already fired up. After we got in his car, he drove at full speed, braking hard in front of my house. He reminded me of a cowboy, and his weapons were his eyes.

The workers were sitting on the lawn, waiting for me to return. Their resting position only confirmed Dad's suspicions and increased his resentment. He swung the sledgehammer high in the air and slammed it to the ground inches from the men's feet. "You put this hammer exactly in the same place when you're done," he shouted. "Are any of you intelligent enough to understand what I said?"

My ears were burning. "Have a bit more respect and stop yelling at the guys," I shouted at Dad. I tried to make him understand that I had offered to get the sledgehammer in the first place.

One of the men thanked my father but received a linked strand of swear words in return. "Who is this man?" another worker asked.

His question was all I needed to get back at Dad. "This man is my father. Would you believe it? He's stupid and he's crazy and he's my father."

"Watch your tongue," Dad warned me, a "how-dare-you" expression frozen on his face. "I'm still your father."

But nothing was going to stop me. "Get out of here now. I hate you!" I walked right up to him. "Get lost!" At my mention of the F word, Dad spun around and left.

The workers laughed and applauded. I felt as if I had performed on stage and the spectators were showing their appreciation. Dad's horrid behavior had given me an opportunity to release my anger and it felt good for a change, but I didn't want to make a habit out of swearing at him.

When the workers completed the job, one of them slammed the sledgehammer in the exact spot my father had pointed out earlier. Everyone laughed and clapped—including me.

Chapter 27
To Love and to Cherish

I had put it off for months, but the pain of a toothache finally forced me to go and see a dentist. After he had tried to freeze my gums for the third time with no success, he asked a doctor in the adjacent office for advice. They agreed the best thing to do was to put me to sleep to remove the four teeth. I wondered how I'd explain my lengthy absence to Sam but went ahead with the procedure anyway.

Because I was groggy after the extraction, the dentist accompanied me home in a taxi. I was late, but the fact that my head was leaning against the dentist's shoulder when the taxi pulled up to the house irritated Sam all the more. He told me he was hungry, snapped his fingers, and demanded a meal. I grabbed the frying pan and put it on the stove.

Sam made sure he had a full stomach before he used his energy to teach me a lesson. I had humiliated him once again, and I knew what that meant. The rape forced me to swallow enormous amounts of blood that made me vomit afterward.

The next morning, Sam had a hangover and life went on as usual.

#

Friends occasionally invited Sam and me to their ski resort not far from home. One evening, I sat alone at a table in the nearby club, singing to the music and absorbing the laughter. Sam sat at the bar next to a woman. Their flirting caught everyone's attention as his hands roamed all over her body. Everyone's eyes were on me, but I didn't move or say a word.

Soon Sam and the woman staggered to my table. "Don't you

find her sexy?" Sam asked me. He placed his hands close to her breasts and glanced from her body to mine. "I'm not dancing with you because you're too tall, skinny, and ugly." He laughed in my face and walked away.

I had heard these remarks so often that I was beginning to believe them. I examined her short plump figure and compared it with mine, which was one hundred and twenty-five pounds spread over a five-foot-six frame. I felt like a pressure cooker that was about to explode, but I held back and smiled at those who were looking my way.

Another dance and the chemistry between Sam and the woman grew more intense as he lifted her up, sat her on the bar, and locked lips with her. I sensed the tension in the air but stayed glued to my seat. An image of Dad during one of his violent rages kept me from blowing up in anger.

The minutes dragged on until the club closed and it was time to leave. Sam and I slowly descended the long stairway with the last of the intoxicated patrons. Then I lost control. I raised my arm high in the air and rammed my purse on Sam's head, over and over again.

Sam ran down the steps and stood laughing at the bottom of the staircase. His laugh wasn't sincere, but it hid his humiliation. Everyone around us thought it was a joke. When I arrived home, I realized otherwise.

The next morning, I was numb with pain and promised Sam that I'd never humiliate him in public again. I went to the washroom to take a shower and smiled when I opened my purse. My mirror, eyeliner, comb—everything was broken, and a tube of hand cream had ruptured and spread over the lining of my purse. Sam hadn't admitted it, of course, but I must have hit him quite hard.

We were invited to the lodge again. It was a carbon copy of the week before as I sat drinking soda pop and singing to the music in the club. At one point, I went to the washroom and shut the door behind me, just to have it pushed open.

Sam was furious about something. He locked the door behind him. "What do you think you're doing?"

"What?"

"I saw you singing and laughing. Who did you see that you want to go to bed with this time?"

"Nobody."

He grabbed me and started to kiss me with frenzy, sucking on my lips and biting them until they bled. "Now you won't feel like kissing anyone," he said.

Just then, the owners of the club—a man and his wife—knocked on the bathroom door. When Sam opened it, they saw me bent over the toilet.

Sam pretended to stroke my head. "Everything is fine. She's drunk again. I'll take care of her."

The owners nodded and left. Like most of our friends, they adored Sam, but because he had such a volatile temper, they feared him as well and didn't meddle in his affairs.

Sam yanked me up. He pulled my hair out in handfuls while he repeated that I mustn't think anyone could ever be attracted to me. I muffled my screams so that no one would hear—something I had learned to master out of necessity if I didn't want the beatings to intensify. Sam made sure I understood that I was never to have such thoughts about men again. Then he swung my head against the toilet seat and walked out.

After I had cleaned myself up, I walked out into the hallway. Sam was waiting for me. He smiled at passers-by while he discreetly held my hand and my wrist behind my back and twisted them in opposite directions, pulling them apart.

Sam thought no one had noticed what he had done to me. But my girlfriend, the owner's wife, had been standing in the hallway behind us and had seen everything. She later pointed to a white line between my wrist and my hand and told me she was sure the joints had come apart.

I was convinced that now was the time to leave Sam. I stood up and headed toward the exit, not aware that he was watching me. I ran down the long stairway, with Sam and the owner in hot pursuit.

"Quick, grab her!" Sam shouted. "She's drunk and out of control. I need to get her home."

They grabbed me and threw me in the back seat of Sam's car but accidentally tore off the white pleated bottom of my navy skirt. They drove down the hill toward our apartment. I knew what Sam had in store for me, so I opened the car door and threw myself out. I felt no pain and darted for the bushes. When they realized what I had done, they put the car in reverse and went looking for me. But they couldn't see me because I was on my back in the deep ditch.

"Forget about her. She's probably gone home. I'll deal with her later," I heard Sam say. They turned the car around and drove back to the lodge.

I crawled out of the ditch and ran to a friend's place in the trailer park behind my parents' home. Louise and Gustave, a young couple with four boys, had been friends of the family for many years. I banged on their door. When Louise appeared in the entrance, I rushed past her to the bedroom where I hid in the closet. I was terrified and begged them not to let Sam in if he came looking for me.

Gustave called the military doctor from the base. A man with dark piercing eyes and black hair arrived within minutes. I thought he was Sam. I began to tremble and couldn't speak. Gustave and Louise held me down while the doctor gave me a tranquilizer. Then the doctor leaned down to smell my breath a few times. As he examined me, he noticed that clumps of my hair had fallen out. He kept asking me what had happened, but I couldn't answer and just kept staring at his eyes. "Everything will be all right," he said.

How can everything be all right when I didn't know what was happening?

There was a knock at the door. It was Sam.

I screamed and crawled back to the closet.

Sam yelled out, "I know she's in there. I just want to bring her home. She's an alcoholic. I always have this problem with her when she drinks."

The doctor knew otherwise. Everyone began to argue. Louise and Gustave finally convinced Sam that I'd spend the rest of the night with them. Either I'd go home the next day or they'd bring me to the hospital.

Sam agreed to leave. "I don't know what all the commotion is about. I never laid a hand on my wife in my life," he shouted in an obvious attempt to hide his guilt.

The next morning, the mirror revealed my true reflection—blasé—as if I didn't care about anything anymore. My hair had thinned and I had multiple bandages on my face, arms, and legs. My garter belt held shreds of nylon stockings. I was wearing half a dress. I sat at the kitchen table, sipping coffee, wondering if the night before had been real or only a bad dream. I could feel the pain and see the damage, but I slipped into a state of denial. I couldn't leave my children, so where else could I go but home?

Sam looked at me as if he had no recollection of last night and snapped his fingers. Even though I was a non-smoker, I hurried to light a cigarette for him and pour his coffee. I didn't want to break the thou-shalt-not-disobey-your-husband rule. Experience had taught me that the punishment in this life was worse than any I could ever imagine in the next.

Chapter 28
Charades

A few nights later, Sam came home from work and handed me an unwrapped present. "I'm sorry I treated you so badly."

I opened the box to find a beautiful cameo pendant. I was ecstatic and wore it every chance I had. I showed it off to everyone and made sure they knew it was a gift from Sam. My grandmother had had a cameo, and every time I saw one, it brought back sweet memories of her.

Sam invited a friend over to watch TV one evening. After they had drunk several large bottles of beer, Sam grabbed my arm and pulled me aside. He told me that tonight was the night that I had to go to bed with his friend. I was to spend no more than fifteen minutes in our bedroom.

I pulled away. I glimpsed the disgusting smirk on his friend's face as he stood up and yanked on his trousers, ready to keep his end of the bargain like the real man he thought he was. The anger inside me surfaced. "Like hell I will, you bunch of retards! Like hell I will!" I reached for a bottle of beer and smashed it on the floor.

Sam and his friend stared at the beer flowing across the living room floor. I waited for a reaction and instantly obtained one.

"You think you're smart, don't you?" Sam said. "Watch this." He smashed the second bottle of beer on the floor.

I picked the last bottle off the table and repeated the gesture.

The men stared at me in awe. "Maybe this wasn't such a good idea," Sam's friend said as he rushed toward the door, with Sam on his heels.

After I shut the door behind them, I thought about what I had done. It had taken guts. No doubt about it, my backbone had definitely strengthened. I felt proud of myself as I turned in for the night, only to be awakened hours later by an irate man who was willing to do anything to make me feel sexy in bed.

And again, it was all in vain. I turned off my mind so that I'd feel nothing as he made love to my unresponsive body. His obscenities surfaced once it was over, as did the throbbing pain from his beatings. I didn't know why they called it "making love." To me, it was a very dark side of my private life.

During happier moments, I lived in dreams of the children and me, laughing and running wild in happy places. Every so often, I wasn't even sure if they were dreams or just wishful thinking.

Sam decided to take me out one night, so I wore the cameo. We sat in the club of the hotel where he worked. He began to flirt with a girl sitting across the room and it bothered me.

"See that girl sitting there all by herself?" Sam asked me.

"Yes."

"I want you to go to the washroom, pass by her table, and invite her to sit with us."

Her face seemed familiar but I wasn't sure. "Why? I don't even know her."

"Just do it."

I went up to her and asked, "Are you alone?"

"Yes, I am," she answered.

"Would you like to join us at our table?"

Before I could finish my sentence, she was already sitting next to Sam. They began to flirt with each other right away.

I interrupted them, breaking the spell they were in. Like a child, I asked her if she had noticed the beautiful cameo pendant Sam had given me.

She glanced at it and laughed. "That's the pendant I gave you for her, isn't it?"

"Yes," Sam replied, chuckling.

Neither one of them blinked when I yanked the chain off, threw it in her face, and left. They didn't even ask me to stay.

On my way home, vague memories surfaced of a woman who had sat at a bar with Sam not long ago. Only then did I realize it was the same woman I had seen kissing him at the ski resort.

Sam didn't come home that night but called every hour to make sure I was there. His mistress took pleasure in adding her final remarks before hanging up, if only to accentuate the fact that they were together. But I didn't mind. If she enjoyed his brutality during sex, I wasn't going to interfere. Better her than me.

Between working as paymaster during the day and dealing with Sam's unpredictability at night, the tension proved more than I could handle. I made an unhealthy decision. I stole cigarettes from Sam's pack and secretly began to smoke. I didn't steal any of the ones I found inside the pockets of his shirts, though. They were twisted at both ends and the tobacco looked too dry. I removed them and put them away until he asked for them.

I welcomed the days when Sam was too drunk to have sex. I would sit alone, listen to music, and imagine how our lives might have turned out differently. I could still make Sam smile when liquor hadn't drenched his thinking. He knew I loved him, and he loved me too. The intensity of our feelings drew us together like magnets. But Sam's inability to make me enjoy sex ate away at his pride. His jealousy prevented him from stepping back and seeing that maybe he was going about it the wrong way.

When I was upset with Sam, I was cautious and avoided mentioning words like crazy, nuts, or insane because they set off a bomb inside him. Over time, I learned to erase them from my vocabulary but used more subtle ways to show my anger.

It was Sam's birthday and I was upset with him, but I hugged him and kissed him anyway. "Happy birthday, Sam," I said and pointed to his gift on the floor.

He smiled when he saw the oversized box topped with a big orange bow. Like a kid, he hurried to unwrap it but had to remove sheet upon sheet of colorful paper before he could get to it. Disappointment swept over his face at the sight of the pumpkin. I was glad I had another gift for him.

#

I often asked Sam for his permission to go to the theater with a girlfriend, but he always refused. One evening, as he was singing in the bathtub, I called my girlfriend. "If you want to go to the theater tonight, pick me up in ten minutes." I opened the washroom door. "Sam, I'm going to the movies." I rushed out of the house knowing that, by the time he got dressed, I'd be well on my way.

As my girlfriend drove away, I looked back and saw Sam running down the street after the car. He wore nothing but a towel wrapped around his waist. A pang of guilt tore through me, but the desire to go to the theater won out. With three theatres in town, I figured I'd be able to see at least one movie before Sam found me.

I took a seat at the end of a row. The lights dimmed and the movie began. I leaned back to get more comfortable but was instantly plucked out of my seat and pushed toward the back of the theater. I fell on my face on the way out. Sam grabbed me and flung me into the back seat of the car.

Sneaking away from Sam had felt good, but the consequences weren't worth it. I tried to explain to him why I had left like that, but no reason would satisfy him. He made me promise that I'd never do it again. In the back of my mind, I promised I'd never run off to the movies while he was in the bathtub, but that was it.

My friend called the next day and said she'd rather stay away from me when Sam was around. I wasn't surprised.

A few days later, Sam woke me from a deep sleep. He told me to hurry up and get dressed.

"What's wrong? What's going on?" I asked as I dressed.

"Go outside and talk to her. She's parked in front of the house."

I looked outside and saw a familiar red car. "What am I supposed to say to her?" I didn't hide the sarcasm in my voice.

Without a word, Sam pushed me out the back door.

I stood shivering next to her car, wondering what I was doing there.

A few moments passed before she rolled down the window. I couldn't help but notice how tired she looked. The blank expression in her eyes told me she was as stunned as I was. "Get in my car," she said. "We need to talk."

"Not unless you give me your keys," I said.

She threw them at me.

As I sat down next to her, I caught a whiff of her perfume. The same scent was embedded in Sam's shirts after he had been with her.

"I can't understand why Sam is still with you." She stared at me with hatred in her eyes. "He doesn't love you. He loves me. Look at you. You have nothing to offer a man. He's hanging onto you because of pity. Give him his freedom."

She was trying to appear confident, but I detected nervousness in her voice. I glanced at the house. Sam was peeking through the curtains. "You want him? Take him. I won't interfere," I said, playing along. "If he loves you so much, why does he always have sex with me after he's been with you?"

My question drew daggers from her eyes.

Suddenly Sam opened the car door. "What are you two talking about?" He forced a chuckle.

I stared at him. "What in the name of God do you think your wife and mistress could be talking about?" I had had enough of their silly charade. I stepped out of the car and took Sam's face in my hands. "Come with me or drive off with her."

He looked into my eyes for a long moment, kissed me, then got in the car, and rode away.

What kind of game was he playing with me? I was so confused, that I started to cry.

Three days later, Sam walked in and put his arms around me. "I want to be with you. I love you."

For the first time, he made love to me without hurting me. But because my feelings in that sector were non-existent, I separated myself as usual from the physical aspect of the act. When Sam cried and told me he didn't want to hurt me, I didn't know what to believe anymore.

Later I tried to sort out what Sam had said. I wondered if he had told me the truth this time. My thoughts were interrupted by a loud scream in the boys' bedroom.

Matthew and Andrew were having a fistfight on the lower bunk bed. Matthew had been sleeping on the upper bunk bed and had dreamed he was a parachutist. He had taken a dive between the wall and the bed, and had landed on top of Andrew, who happened to be dreaming that wolves were attacking him. After I calmed the boys down, they went back to bed.

When the phone rang that night, Sam answered. It was his mistress. He pointed a finger at me. "Sit on the chair and listen to this," he ordered. "Her? I wouldn't touch her with a ten-foot pole.

She's ugly and skinny, and I have no desire to make love to her."

I looked at Sam in disbelief. "You're both insane and belong together," I yelled at him and stood up.

Sam dropped the phone and pushed me back into the chair. "You listen to every word I say." He continued to talk about sex with his mistress but never took his eyes off me.

I grabbed the phone and, in one breath, I asked her about the baby boy she had given away and about her stretch marks. I told her how Sam had said her stomach looked like a cobblestone path, then he yanked the phone from my hand.

Sam had trouble convincing her that I had made up these stories because he knew they were true. He had divulged them to me during one of his rare honest moments.

The next morning, I was sitting at the kitchen table when Sam walked in, smiled, and winked at me as if everything was okay between us. I was in awe at his nonchalant attitude but more confused about mine. Did I or didn't I care about him? Had he hurt my heart or my pride? While he was with his mistress, I could catch my breath, stand tall, and wait for the next blow. On the other hand, his unfaithfulness was destroying our marriage. "I don't care what you say or what you do anymore, Sam. One day, I'm going to stop loving you."

"You will always love me," he shouted.

From then on, my love for him gradually disintegrated to the point where I felt nothing emotionally, only complete indifference. I shed the fear and guilt that had kept me in a world of self-pity, hatred, and panic for so long and began to search for my inner worth. Enjoying a sunrise or watching the moon surrounded by a star-covered sky was like a first-time experience for me. Had they always been there? I marveled when a breeze filled my lungs with the perfume of flowers. How could I have been entangled in a web so tight that I couldn't see the beauty of nature all around me?

I had a secret, but I wouldn't tell anyone. I had overcome Sam's repeated schemes to drown my enthusiasm and break my spirit, and it felt terrific. I spent days on end thinking of ways to leave him. I'd have left in a heartbeat if I could have found a solution that included my children. But there was no escape for me and I fell into the deepest pit of despair.

I sat alone in the middle of the night when sleep wouldn't come and serenity filled the air. During those times, I believed that I was on the brink of insanity. In desperation, I'd get on my knees and pray, *"God, if you can hear me, please help me. Please cast a spell over me that will enable me to sleep until I'm old and gray."* I didn't want to live through my thirties, forties, and fifties. I sincerely believed that, if I prayed hard enough, anything was possible.

Lack of sleep, too much coffee, and too many cigarettes were taking their toll on me. Luckily, the children kept me sane. We went for months during the winter without electricity in the house. I couldn't afford to pay all the bills on my salary alone, and I had no help from Sam because his "entertainment" expenses exceeded his income. Aside from the occasional warm meal at Mom's and foodstuff that Dad placed inside my front door from time to time, the children and I had to rely on cold porridge, cold soup, and other cold meals.

Every evening, the children gathered at the kitchen table and I helped them with their homework. But even as they played, I could see the pain behind the gaze of their innocent eyes. We slept in the same bed to keep warm, and I read them a fairy tale before the last of three candles died out. When worries kept me awake at night, I watched the cool breaths of air exhaling from their little mouths and fell asleep to the sound of their growling stomachs. I never understood how they managed to get through this harsh period in their lives, but if it weren't for them, I know I wouldn't have survived.

Chapter 29
Dance

Sam woke me up one night with another brilliant idea. He wanted me to go to the club at the hotel where he worked the following evening. A few of his friends' wives would be there. He didn't want me to drink or dance but just sit there with them and act normal—whatever that meant. I insisted that I didn't want to go but, as usual, he ignored me.

People stared at me as I walked into the club. Everyone knew of Sam's affairs with other women, but they had never seen me at the hotel. I wore a white bohemian blouse with a soft flowing skirt—the kind I felt the most comfortable in. I wore no makeup and let my long hair hang loose.

I was sitting at the table sipping a soda pop and listening to the music, when a man came up to me. "Would you care to dance?"

"Sorry, no thank you," I said, without even looking at him. I refused requests to dance from other men as well.

The waiter arrived with a message that Sam wanted to see me, so I walked over to where he was sitting at the bar.

Sam leaned over and whispered in my ear, "I want you to dance. All you're doing is sitting there looking stupid. You don't drink or smoke, so act like a woman and at least dance."

He gazed into my eyes but the lights were dim, so I couldn't tell if he was lying or not. "You actually want me to dance?" I asked him.

"Yes, I do."

"Why didn't you tell me before? Now all the guys have already asked and I refused." I turned and walked back to my table.

I was debating if what Sam had said was sincere or not, when I heard, "Will you dance with me?" A tall man in tight jeans and a red tee shirt greeted me with a beautiful smile. Curly blond hair and blue eyes set off a tanned skin.

I was on my feet in an instant. "Yes, I will. Thank you."

We danced to rock-and-roll music. The next dance was a slow one, so he pulled me close to him. I found the scent of his lotion attractive. Why did dancing with him feel so good? As we drifted into the next song, I glanced at the bar and saw Sam waving his arms in the air. He wanted me to sit down, but I decided I'd finish the dance first, so I turned my back to him.

The young man ran his fingers along my neck and told me how much he loved women's necks. I felt uneasy and looked in Sam's direction again. He was kneeling on the bar, waving his arms to get my attention. I made a bad choice: I continued to dance.

In the next instant, Sam clutched my arm. His eyes were on fire and his lips were purple and trembling. "I knew you'd dance, even though you knew I really didn't want you to. You look like a whore. If it's a divorce you want, I'll give it to you."

By this time, my dancing partner had vanished and the music had stopped. Sam and I were alone on the dance floor, and all eyes were on us. Some women were laughing; others looked concerned or curious as to what would happen next.

I ran to the washroom. Sam was right behind me. He pushed me into a corner but lost his grip on me, so I ran out the door. Why had he told me to dance? When would I ever learn?

At five in the morning, Sam stood in front of me in the bedroom. I knew what to expect. He put his hand over my mouth. His breath smelled of cigarettes and alcohol. "Is this what you think it would have been like?" he yelled. When he was done, he rolled over and fell asleep.

Days later, he blurted out, "If any of the women ask you to go out with them, I want you to refuse. I don't ever want to see you at the hotel again. Understood?" He poked my forehead to reinforce every word he said.

But months later, Sam had a different proposition. "I'm so sorry that I've treated you badly."

Where was this remorse coming from? What was he up to this time?

He sat on the sofa next to me and held my hand. "You have my permission to go out with a girlfriend if you want." His voice didn't sound normal.

"No, I don't want to go out." I stood up, but he pulled me back down and insisted that I listen to him.

"It's not often that I give you permission to go out, so you might as well take advantage of my generosity."

"What's wrong with you? It's eleven o'clock. No one wants to go out this late."

"Your neighbor next door might. I saw the light on over there."

Sandy and I had been friends for a few years. She was a free woman and enjoyed going to bars and dancing. I had refused her invitations to go out even though the idea had been tempting at times. "No." I started to walk toward the bedroom.

"Call her and ask her." He handed me the phone.

I dialed her number. "Hi, it's Diane. Do you feel like going to the Chateau tonight?"

"Is he home?" she whispered.

"Yes."

Sam held the phone to his ear so he could listen to our conversation.

"He's there? Is he nuts or something? Be careful."

I looked at Sam, not knowing what to say.

He nodded for me to go on.

"Do you want to go out or not, Sandy?" I asked.

"Yeah, sure. I'll pick you up in fifteen minutes." She hung up.

Sam didn't get angry about Sandy's comments. Instead he spoke very slowly and clearly. "Get ready. You can go to the hotel, but you have to be home by midnight."

I felt like Cinderella. "Never mind. It's already eleven-thirty." I picked up the phone to cancel my outing.

"Ok, ok, twelve-thirty then." Sam seemed impatient.

It was a five-minute drive to the nightclub. Sandy's brother, John, worked at the sawmill and had stopped at the club right after his shift to have a few beers. He was a tall, clumsy guy with protruding teeth. He hadn't bothered to change, so his clothes reeked with the odor of a hard day's work. Regardless, I didn't hesitate when he asked me to dance with him. Sam wasn't around and John was nothing to be jealous about anyway.

As a slow dance came on, I noticed Sam in the doorway. I turned my back on him and continued to dance with John. Same scenario, same mistake.

Sam came up to me and insisted that I stop dancing, so I sat down at the table. "I'll wait for you at the door," he said.

What had I done? Why had I fallen for Sam's game again?

"You'll be safe as long as you stay here." Sandy pointed with her chin to three plainclothes policemen sitting at the bar. Sam's loud persistence had caught their attention and they glanced at us now and then.

I didn't know what to do, so I remained seated.

Minutes later, Sam returned. "I want you to come with me. Now."

I grabbed my sweater and fumbled with it, then threw it in his face and ran out the door. It surprised him and gave me a head start. I ran across the street to the police station. Just as I reached for the door handle, Sam pulled me to the ground. Within seconds, police officers surrounded us and asked us what was going on.

Sam replied right away, "She's my wife and she's drunk. I just want to bring her home."

But I didn't want to go home. Sam was in a tight spot and had been humiliated. The consequences of my silence could only prove devastating for me. The fear of going against the thou-shalt-not-disobey-your-husband rule instantly lost its priority. "Please don't send me home with him," I pleaded with the police officers. "I'm afraid. Please don't send me home." I was searching for a sign of compassion in their eyes when I noticed a familiar face.

An officer who lived in the apartment on a floor above us recognized us and said, "Come into the station, and we'll set things straight."

I was relieved—at least for a while. Sam and I sat in a tiny room while two officers questioned us. Sam reassured them that he'd never hurt me and that he knew exactly what to do with me when I was drunk. But his argument didn't convince them. They took him aside and questioned him in private. Then it was my turn.

I told them how I ended up at the Chateau. How Sam gave me

permission to go out that night. I told them that I didn't drink alcohol. I couldn't tell if they believed me or not. "Please don't send me home with him. I'm sure something terrible will happen to me. I'm so tired of everything—the beatings, the threats, and his mistress. I'm tired of having no food for the children. I'm so fed up with life that I don't care any more." I began to cry.

The officers detained us until morning, which worked out to my advantage. I didn't like intruding on my parents or my friends while they slept, so I often had no place to escape to at night when Sam let loose his wrath.

A police officer put Sam and me in the same room and asked us to settle our differences. Alone with me again, Sam began to pull my hair, but little did he know that my scalp had grown numb to his ritual and it didn't hurt anymore. "Why did you go out in the first place? Can't you see what happens when you disobey?"

"You told me to go out."

"I was just testing you. Didn't you know that? I knew you'd go out." To make certain that I understood, he pounded my forehead with his finger and began to knuckle my face. He twisted my arms, then pulled them backwards. The door opened, and Sam hastily switched to caressing me and telling me how much he loved me. The police would check in on us once in a while, but all they could see was a caring husband who was genuinely concerned about his wife.

The sun was rising and a beautiful day was beginning. The police officer who lived in our building came in and asked if we were ready to go home. He looked straight into Sam's eyes and said, "Don't put a finger on her. My shift is over, so I'm going home. Don't touch her. Do you understand?"

"I've never touched my wife in my life. What do you think I am? I love her so much," Sam said. He put his arm around my waist and kissed me on the cheek. I turned my head away. His fingers were digging into my side, but I remained silent.

I could feel the tension building up in Sam as we drove home. I was praying that he'd follow the police officer's order. I made breakfast for the children before they left for school. As I shut the door behind them, Sam slapped me to the ground. He dragged me to the bedroom and placed a pillow over my face to muffle any sounds I'd make. I formed pockets of air between the pillow and me so I could breathe.

After it was over, Sam walked out of the bedroom. He sat at the table and snapped his fingers. I made his breakfast and lit him a cigarette.

#

We moved from the apartment and rented a two-story stone house. The bedrooms were all upstairs, except for the master bedroom on the first floor.

Sam and his mistress were still quite involved. They ate in restaurants and slept in motels while the children and I often went without food or heat. Mom often asked me how things were going, but I didn't tell her because she had enough worries of her own.

When I was alone at home, getting rid of the stress within me took on the utmost importance. I danced to loud music—any type of music—because it improved my movements and mood after only a few minutes. I swirled around and around and pretended to be a gypsy who was as free as the wind and full of mischief. My taste for long flared skirts, peasant blouses, and going barefoot added to my fantasy of a passionate bohemian. Bold black eyeliner and a flower in my hair enhanced the appearance of my imaginary self. I danced and twirled until I visualized all the hurt, negativity, and stress roll off my body. Exhausted and rid of the tension within me, I'd slump to the floor.

Chapter 30
Tragedy Strikes Again

Nanette's memories of Christmas were pleasant, as she had often pointed out to her husband, and she looked forward to celebrating her first Christmas in years with the rest of her siblings and their families.

We had gathered in the living room of our parents' home on Christmas Eve. Dad was drunk and angry. Out of the blue, he insulted and degraded Timmy's wife. Dad sat with his head in his hands as we had seen him do many times before and began to curse. The atmosphere soon turned sour and everyone grew wary, wondering what Dad's next move would be. Nanette and her family hurried upstairs and huddled together on a bed, her dream of a happy family reunion wiped out within seconds. The occasion ruined any chance of future Christmas get-togethers at our parents' home.

#

It was summer and I hadn't seen my younger brother Billy in six months. I called him and we made plans to meet at Nanette's the following Friday.

Thursday crawled by so slowly—probably because I was eager to give my brother a big hug. When the phone rang, I thought it was Billy and answered with a hearty "Hello!" The elderly man at the other end of the line related the horrible news, but I refused to believe it.

Billy was missing. The day had been warm and sunny, so my brother and a friend had gone sailing. After an afternoon of fun, they overturned the sailboat on purpose, not realizing that bringing it back to its upright position would be difficult. Exhausted from trying to upright the boat, they soon lost track of time. The sun had set and the other sailboats had returned to shore. The sound of fierce rapids in the distance probably warned them they were heading in that direction, so they called out for help.

The old man shouted out to them, "Swim this way. I think you're about thirty yards from shore." He aimed a flashlight in their direction in an attempt to guide them, but he failed to convince them to swim to shore. Then he heard a horrifying scream. Either Billy or his friend had let go and had been washed away by the rapids. "At least try to swim to shore," the man cried out in a panic to the one who remained. "Try, you have nothing to lose."

"I can't let go. I'm exhausted," the weak response came back, but the fierce sound of the rapids broke up their contact.

The old man heard another scream, then silence. When help finally arrived, he was still trying to communicate, but there was no one left in the water. Billy and his friend had been pulled through the rapids. Their chances of survival were nil.

The man was in shock and was brought to the hospital. The family that had wanted to adopt Katie visited him there to hear his story firsthand. Still recovering from the ordeal, the man had difficulty explaining what had happened. Above all, he felt guilty for not having convinced the two young men to swim to shore.

They found Billy nine days later. I'd never see him again or hear the thump in the middle of the night when he ran from Mom's house to mine and asked for a massage. I'd massage the tense muscles of his back for hours and talk until dawn while everyone else slept.

Another funeral. When would it all end? The casket was closed, which made the acceptance of Billy's death almost impossible. A group of students and parents came to his funeral. A close friend of Billy's decided not to come but expressed his grief in the only way he could: he dropped roses from the bridge near where Billy had lost his life.

Just before I entered the funeral parlor, a monarch butterfly fluttered above me and settled on my arm. I immediately thought of how short Billy's life had been but how it had brought a vast amount of love to so many. I was thankful he had rid himself of the horrible secrets that had taunted him his whole life. Billy had a quiet, slow, and melancholic temperament. Any laughter or smile hid the shadow of pain that only a perceptive few could detect.

Mom changed a lot after Billy's death. She had lost her two youngest children. Extreme pain caused her to drift even deeper into her imaginary world. She didn't cry, but her eyes were as empty as her heart and smiles were rare. She didn't talk much but puttered routinely around the house. Dad became more confused and had difficulty in expressing his feelings. He drowned his pain in the only way he knew—the bottle.

Chapter 31
Breaking a Major Thou-shalt-not Rule

Sometimes Sam and I would spend a moment alone, and kiss and giggle like a couple of teenagers in love. His smile and tender touch comforted me, and when we hugged, I wished it would go on forever. The handsome boy who had once called me "black beauty" was still the man I loved. I was certain that no one could make me happier, and I often wondered how different our lives would have been if I had overcome the hurdle of my first sexual experience.

The look in Sam's eyes told me that he was still searching for a solution. One evening, after the children had fallen asleep, we hired a babysitter and went out. We were walking hand in hand down the street, when he suggested we stop at a certain hotel for a drink.

I was surprised. The hotel was a hole frequented by winos that drank themselves into a coma. The place reeked of cigarette smoke, alcohol, and dirty rugs. "Why did you want to come here?" I asked Sam.

He sat me down at a table, went to the bar where a handful of drunks were sitting, and came back with a Seven Up. He stood behind me, placed a few quarters on the table for the jukebox, and whispered in my ear. "I'm leaving you now. I want you to stay. Choose one man and go to bed with him."

I froze. Was I hearing right? I jumped up and started for the door, but Sam grabbed me and pushed me back in the chair.

"You have half an hour to choose a man and have sex with him." Eyes blazing, Sam stared at me to make sure I had understood. Then he walked out.

The mishmash of smells alone made me sick to my stomach. I

glanced around. The men who sat at the bar resembled basset hounds with bloodshot eyes. I put the quarters in the jukebox and punched in the songs: Can't Take My Eyes Off of You, by Frankie Valli; Girl, You'll Be a Woman Soon, by Neil Diamond; and Bobby Vinton's, Please Love Me Forever.

Once I had drowned my pain in the songs, I left the hotel. I noticed a man standing in a phone booth outside. He had a jacket over his head. I shivered when I recognized Sam, but I pretended I hadn't seen him and moved on.

I took the long way home to clear my mind. What was he doing in the phone booth, other than checking up on me? I walked up the stairs to the apartment and opened the door to find Sam sitting at the kitchen table. He was breathing heavy and his lips were dark purple. He had no doubt run all the way home to get here before me, yet he managed to ask me how many men I had had sex with.

I approached him and gently put my hand on his heart. I looked straight into those eyes filled with so many emotions that it was hard to grasp what he was really thinking. "I saw you in the phone booth, Sam."

"That wasn't me. Now answer my question."

"You already know the answer."

He stood up and faced me. "I don't believe you," he shouted.

I was afraid that the police officer who lived in our building would hear him and come down to check on us. I stayed calm and tried to make Sam understand that all I needed was him.

He took me in his arms and told me I was the only one he wanted too, but he believed our lives were in such turmoil that he didn't know how we could go on. "I don't understand why we're having such a hard time. I love you."

Sam had opened up his soul to me. As I pierced my way through his doubts, I tried to reach out to him and love him the way he wanted. If only he knew how intense my love was for him during these rare moments. I would have died for him.

However, the damage was permanent. I loved him but couldn't enjoy sex with him, no matter how hard I tried. It was too rough and painful, and the humiliating things he did to me only added to my anxiety. Fear would invade me and I'd drift to my haven until it was over.

The next night, after Sam had had five beers, he thought it might be fun to scare me while we were having sex. He was convinced that, if he drank, violence during sex would be more acceptable. I supposed he wanted to get a reaction from me because any reaction would have been better than none.

A knife to my throat seemed appropriate as he began his interrogation. I answered each question correctly, as if someone were putting the words in my mouth. The sensation of the cold blade on my neck made me nervous. I pulled it away from me, not realizing I was holding the handle. The knife cut easily through Sam's skin, and his thumb hung loosely from his hand.

I couldn't convince him to go to the hospital. He fell asleep with his hand clenched over his thumb. The next morning, he was confused about what had happened, but I wasn't. I believed that my angels' task was to protect me that night. They did, and I couldn't thank them enough. Neither Sam nor I ever mentioned the incident again.

My calm demeanor and my ability to function and cope with Sam's threats troubled him. After seven years, he was still involved with his mistress. Friends often asked me what I was going to do about his affairs. I replied that I'd rather spend my time with the children anyway. When Sam was with her, at least he wasn't hurting me.

But that wasn't the case. Every time Sam came home smelling of her perfume and makeup, he still had sex with me. It was as if he had to prove that he could still fulfill his marital obligations.

#

Sam wasn't keen on my need to go to confession. As a result, I hadn't been to church since my marriage. Because it wasn't unusual for a priest to come to the house to hear a confession, I requested a visit. "Bless me, father, for I have sinned." There were no stolen candies to confess this time, but I was sure my sins were worse and I'd get no less than a rosary for my penance.

The priest's response to my confession shocked me. "I regret having joined you and Sam in marriage." He took a deep breath. "I wish to annul your marriage because I believe that you and Sam don't belong together."

I was stunned and couldn't imagine why he'd say such a

thing. Maybe my mother had filled his head with ridiculous stories about Sam. "Father, when Sam and I got married, we took vows. We said, 'till death do us part.' It would be a mortal sin to annul the marriage." I shook my head. "No, I don't want you to do it. I love him, and he's my husband."

"Please reconsider," he pleaded.

I thought about the five children I had had with Sam. "There's nothing to reconsider. I won't agree to it."

Chapter 32
Deadly Combination

Daniel was tinier than my other boys but just as beautiful. I never understood why he'd try to wiggle out of my arms when he was a baby. While he was growing up, I sensed that a thin wall stood between us, invisible to anyone else. Daniel's problems were apparent, but even visits to the doctor's office offered no solutions.

From an early age, Daniel had a unique interest that perplexed me, since I had no idea what could have triggered it: he had an obsessive interest in cars. By the age of three, he had acquired an endless curiosity and spent hours dismantling small appliances to see how they worked.

After I had tucked Daniel in bed for a nap one afternoon, sleep crept over me instead. I woke up gasping for air after dreaming that I had been tightened in a vise. Daniel was sitting on my chest with a razor blade in one hand and shaving cream in the other. I didn't move in case I'd scare him, but I stared into his eyes—eyes that were strangely void of expression. "What are you doing?" I asked, keeping my voice calm.

He smiled and showed me handfuls of hair—my hair that he had shaved off!

I was speechless. I tried to get up but couldn't. My arms and legs were tied to the bedspring with polyester wool. I used every tone of voice to persuade Daniel to untie me but he wouldn't.

A few hours later, the older boys arrived home from school. It was probably for the best that I had remained tied up for so long. If Daniel had untied me earlier, God only knew what I would have done to him.

I ran to the bathroom and stared at my reflection in the mirror. Was I having another nightmare? Daniel had shaved off all my hair, except for the back of my head. I was so stunned that I couldn't even get angry. Jokes abounded at the office until my hair began to grow back. I wanted to punish Daniel, but I figured he was too young to have known better. Sam, of course, found *it heristickle*, as he put it.

My hair grew in but I was still upset with Daniel. Every time he'd do something bad, like shave Katherine's hair, I pulled his hair and let go only when I was tempted to lift him up off the floor. But he was always one step ahead of me. He shaved his head.

I brought Daniel to see a doctor again. An ashtray filled with cigarette butts sat on the doctor's desk. Without warning, Daniel let go of my hand. He jumped on a chair and blew as hard as he could into the ashtray, scattering the ashes across the doctor's papers and onto his white medical coat. Daniel then grabbed a cabinet full of little drawers, flung it to the ground, and watched the colorful pills spread across the floor.

I stood up, flabbergasted. The doctor slowly rose out of his chair, changed his soiled white coat for a clean one, and asked me what he could do for me. After I explained the situation, he assured me that "boys will be boys" and that I shouldn't worry. I was being overdramatic, he said, and escorted me to the door.

Waking up at night while everyone was asleep was Daniel's favorite pastime. He would roam the house in darkness looking for his next thrill. One night, he covered the floor with milk and ashes from the fireplace. I stood frozen to the spot as I watched him in action. I snuck back to bed and waited for morning to arrive. "This is not normal," I repeated to myself.

Over the years, Daniel's curiosity increased and made him vulnerable to trouble. Nothing could stop him. His intelligence combined with his inquisitiveness bordered on lethal. In spite of numerous discussions I had had with him ever since he was a young boy, he continued to cause enough damage to boost his chances of joining his friends in reform school. He was like a runaway train with no one at the controls, and the solution to the problem was nowhere to be found.

As Daniel headed toward his teen years, his boredom increased. He was twelve and his obsession for cars had peaked. He asked if he could ride around with me in my car equipped with a standard transmission, then studied every movement I made. I didn't think much of it until I came home for lunch the next day and my car was gone. I noticed a small hole in the glass partition of the front door. I unlocked the door to discover that my home had been ransacked.

When the police arrived, I explained what had happened. One of the police officers stepped forward, looked down the hallway, and said, "I'm sure it was your son, Daniel."

"How dare you accuse my son of such a thing?" I retorted. Yet something in the back of my mind told me he might be right.

I stayed home the rest of the day. I refused to let my frustration get the best of me, so I turned up the volume on the radio and danced as I cleaned up the mess.

When Daniel came back from school, I asked him how his day went. "Not too exciting," he said with a shrug and then started to walk away.

My next question caught him off guard. "Did you enjoy your ride? Where's my car?"

He turned around and smiled. "Your car is in the ditch a few miles away." He didn't appear to be the least bit bothered by it.

"The police were here. They said you stole my car and made this mess."

A smug look swept over his face. "I wanted you to think it was a robbery." He admitted that he was careful not to break the entire window, just a piece big enough to pass his hand through to unlock the door.

His breath smelled of cigarettes, so I offered him one. "How long have you been smoking?"

"Quite a while," he said with a smirk.

He refused my offer of a second cigarette, but I insisted. After he finished it, I could tell he was feeling sick. "I don't ever want to see you with another cigarette in your mouth." I felt awkward because I had a pack. Practice what you preach, I thought.

#

In the hope of finding a better life elsewhere, Sam and I decided to move. With five children and Buddy, our dog, it was impossible to find an apartment, so we settled for a train coach that sat on the side of the road next to a farm. It held a tiny sink with cold running water, a couch, a small table, four shelf-like bunk beds, and a folding bed. This will be great, I thought. The boys could sleep on the bunk beds, and Sam, Katie, and I could use the bed. But something was missing: a washroom. It turned out to be an outhouse tucked in the bushes about a hundred feet from our new home.

Living in the coach didn't turn out to be such a good idea, but we managed to live there for a whole summer. Buddy ran in the fields and snapped at the cows' legs. The farm owner often complained that the dog's barking was souring the cows' milk.

One day, the owner—a short stubby man who always wore a baseball hat to hide his bald head—was driving by and noticed me washing clothes outdoors. In the next instant, he hit the brakes, jumped out, and threw me to the ground—away from the washing machine. I was stunned and unable to speak as he lay on top of me, lines of concern etched across his forehead. He stood up, composed himself, and explained his behavior. He pointed out that I had been standing ankle high in a pool of water with a frayed electrical cord hanging next to me. He proceeded to hammer nails into the side of the coach and secure the cord.

#

Our old Mercedes had huge holes in the floor. When the boys became restless and began to wrestle in the back seat, I'd say three words, "Stand up, boys," and they'd stop.

Sam took a job in sales. After he waved good-bye one morning and drove off to work, I noticed that two of my boys were missing. I ran in every direction calling out their names. Then I caught a hint of guilt in Daniel's eyes. I knelt in front of him and asked, "Where are they?"

He hesitated, then pointed in the direction that Sam had taken to go to work. I assumed that the boys were in the back seat of the car and that Sam would see them and bring them home. But minutes later, Daniel decided to tell me the truth. The boys weren't in the back seat—they were in the trunk.

The car was so rusted that I was afraid they might suffocate. I ran across the street to an attractive red brick house and rang the doorbell. The elderly lady who lived in the two-story building greeted me in big fluffy slippers and huge curlers. She looked like

Carol Burnett, the comedian, who used to dress the same way in her TV skits. I explained what had happened and begged her to help me. We jumped into her car and drove off.

We were approaching the highway when we spotted a police car. I bounded out of the car, and waved and screamed to get the officer's attention. After I explained my dilemma, the officer immediately contacted other patrol cars and the hunt was on.

When the police pulled Sam aside, they asked him to open the trunk. "I think you might have a couple of children in there," the officer told him.

Upset by the delay, Sam exploded in anger. "I'll eat my shirt if there are children in there."

"Bang, bang," Matthew said as the trunk opened. Next to him was Charlie, half asleep.

Sam drove up the driveway. He stepped out, opened the back door, threw the boys out, and drove off without a word.

Chapter 33
Silent Exit

In the fall, life took on a familiar rhythm. We moved back to our hometown and rented a three-room apartment.

One evening after Sam had gone out and the children were asleep, I examined the pattern of events in my life. I determined that my self-esteem and integrity had been chipped away to nothing, and my reason for living wasn't clear anymore. I decided that I had had enough.

I asked the doctor to prescribe something to help me sleep. He understood the turmoil in my life and gave me thirty sleeping pills. He had made me promise that I wouldn't do anything silly.

Before Sam had left to spend the weekend with his mistress, he had told me it was useless to stay home with someone as unattractive as me. Alone in the silence of night, my heart wept while my children's silent breaths filled the room. I opened the container and swallowed the sleeping pills one at a time until there were no more.

I sat still, not quite grasping the extent of my deed. I started to talk out loud, regretting what I had done, wondering how I could reverse the last half hour, but the medication had already begun to blur my thoughts.

All of a sudden, Sam walked in. His trip had been delayed and he had returned for a bite to eat. I shrugged off a drowsy feeling and went to the kitchen to prepare food. I was functioning in slow motion and nothing seemed real.

Sam watched me fumble with the dishes. He stared at me, as if he were trying to understand what was wrong with me. Then he went to the living room and found the empty container of pills sitting on the corner table. "What have you done?" he shouted, shaking me.

But the more he shook me, the more I laughed, and the greater his fear became. I felt no pain. I hadn't experienced such an overpowering urge to sleep in so long that I welcomed the feeling of complete relaxation.

"Did you take all the pills?" he asked me.

"I didn't take them." I paused. "You gave them to me."

He swept me up in his arms and carried me to the car.

At the hospital, I was vaguely aware of my surroundings. I heard Sam talking to the hospital staff, explaining that I had overdosed on sleeping pills. As they rushed me to the emergency ward, I fell in and out of sleep, certain that it was too late and that it would soon be over. Then someone asked me why I had taken the pills. I replied that Sam had given them to me.

The hospital staff forced three containers of a dark substance down my throat. I was dead set on keeping it inside, but an uncontrollable reaction brought the liquid gushing out in one huge blast. I heard someone say I was out of danger.

Nurses and doctors scurried around as Sam tried over and over to explain to them that he wasn't to blame for my condition. One of the staff ordered him to go and sit down, but he kept pacing around. Then they called security.

"Please tell them the truth!" Sam yelled at me.

I wasn't going to die, so I knew I had to rectify the situation. The frantic look on Sam's face made me feel guilty for having put him through such an ordeal, so I confessed.

Sam let out a sigh of relief. He looked at me. "What have I done that you would want to die?" The expression in his eyes told me he was sincere.

"It's because I love you. I can't make you happy and I don't want to be with anybody else," I said, crying. But how could I expect him to understand?

The next morning, I returned home. Sam and I didn't speak for several hours until he asked, "Why did you do it?"

"I'm sorry for having caused you pain," I said. "I'm so tired of life and I'm of no use to you. No matter how hard I try, I can't love you the way you want, and I don't want to love anyone else." I couldn't stop crying. "I'm afraid I can't take care of the children. I don't understand why our life is such a mess."

Mixed emotions surfaced as we sat, crying and hugging each other, not wanting to let go. We agreed that all odds were against us and that we couldn't see a way out of our predicament. We were trapped.

A week later, my doctor made an appointment for me to see a psychiatrist. As I sat in the psychiatrist's office, I glanced out the window and noticed a shed on the grounds.

The psychiatrist, who was observing every move I made, asked me what I was looking at.

"I see a man hanging there. I think Sam's hanging over there," I replied, pointing to the shed. Within seconds, everything changed. The air hung thick and heavy, and I couldn't breathe. "Do something! Please help Sam. I don't understand why he's hanging there." I broke down and cried. "Why is he hanging from there? What's happening?" I shouted. "Please put me in the hospital. I promise I won't cause any trouble. I'll even help with the cleaning." The next breath became more desperate than the last.

But the psychiatrist encouraged me to keep talking. It was exactly what I needed: someone to talk to, someone who would listen. So I told him everything. When I had finished, he asked, "How are you feeling?"

I was amazed at the relief I felt. As I spoke, I became more and more relaxed. I didn't see Sam hanging in the shed any more. All I wanted to do was be with him and start over again.

The psychiatrist made me understand that he didn't want to put me in the hospital. He preferred to speak with Sam and wanted me to make an appointment for him. I told the doctor that it would be impossible. Besides, Sam didn't need help. I was the troubled one. The doctor escorted me to the door and reassured me that it was indeed Sam he wanted to see.

When I told Sam about the psychiatrist's request, he said, "What have you done? Why did you go see a doctor—a psychiatrist at that? If you're crazy, that's one thing. Admit yourself to a mental hospital, but leave me out of it." He made a phone call. "I'm going out for a drink." He slammed the door behind him.

Why did he have to lie to me? I knew he was going to meet

his girlfriend. Then again, I wondered if I wasn't assuming the worst about him. Maybe he was just going out for a drink. To put my mind at ease, I decided to follow him.

When I saw Sam entering a bar, I hated myself for having doubted him. I turned around and was heading down Main Street when I saw Sam running in a back alley. I thought someone was chasing him, so I ran in the same direction. When I reached the end of the street, I saw his girlfriend waiting for him in her red car.

Sam came dashing from the back alley toward her car but saw me and stopped. He walked up to me and put his arms around me. "What are you doing here?" His voice was shaky.

"What are you doing? What is she doing? Where are you going?" I bombarded him with questions.

"You're hallucinating. No one else is here. I was just going to the tavern for a beer."

I glanced at his girlfriend. She met my gaze with a smirk. Suddenly I felt so alone. I didn't want him to go with her. I wanted him to stay with me. I walked up to her car and asked her to roll down the window. She refused. Then I lost it. I grabbed Sam by the arms and pleaded, "Tell her to go away! Come home with me Sam!"

He put his arms around my shoulders as before and led me away from the car. "There's no one there. You're hallucinating. You need help."

"But I can see her. What's going on, Sam? Why are you doing this to me?" I began to cry. "If you don't want to be with me or the family, just tell me and I'll leave you alone."

He walked me home. When we arrived, he said he was going back out for a beer and insisted I stay in the house. He looked back at me and shook his head, then walked out the door.

I waited a few seconds and then hurried to get to the corner before he did. I was standing in front of his girlfriend's car when a man walked by. I stopped him and asked him to tell me the color of the car behind me.

The man said, "It's a red car, and a lady with long blond hair is sitting inside." He told me more than I had expected.

I was sitting on the car when the roadrunner arrived again, but this time he looked exhausted. "A man confirmed that I'm not sitting on a rock," I told Sam. "She's waiting for you, so please tell me the truth."

"You think you see something? You think you see a car? Does it look as if I'm getting in a car? You're sick and you need help. Go home." He shut the door and they rode away.

I felt sad about the whole incident but was relieved that I hadn't imagined it. Sam was either punishing me for having seen the psychiatrist or was trying to make me believe I was delusional so that I'd have no valid reason to leave him.

I opened the front door and the phone was ringing. Sam wanted to make sure I had gone straight home. It was strange how sleep came easy that night, aside from the fact that his phone calls woke me up every hour. "Just checking. I don't want you to go out," he'd say. I had no intention of going out and he knew it, but he kept calling me all the same.

However, one phone call did prevent me from falling asleep. With laughter in her voice, his girlfriend reassured me that she'd take good care of him. "I must be doing something right because he keeps coming back to me," she snickered.

Three days passed and Sam still hadn't come home.

Luckily, my full-time job helped me to focus on other matters. Because employment was booming, I left my old job at the mine and found a new one closer to home at a construction company. My employer's compassion toward the staff and their mutual respect for him convinced me that I had made a good choice.

The first call I took was from a man who said," I do erections." I slammed the receiver down. "I can't believe it," I said out loud.

The boss heard me and asked, "What was that about?"

"It's just one of those calls." I thought my boss would let it go at that, but he insisted that I tell him what the caller had said. "It was an obscene call. The man said he did erections, so I hung up."

My boss paused for a moment, then smiled and explained how that word was part of the terminology used in the construction industry. I had just learned a word that I wasn't about to forget.

One day, as two men walked into the office, a gust of wind blew the papers on the counter into the air. As I tried to catch them, I bent over and didn't notice the spiky message holder sitting on the desk. I felt a pain in my breast but wasn't about to let anyone know. I stood up straight and looked at the men as if to say, "Couldn't you have been more careful?"

With stunned expressions on their faces, they stared at my face and breast.

I thought I had a stain on my blouse, so I glanced down. The paper holder had entered my breast and was hanging from my chest. All of a sudden, excruciating pain pounded in my breast. I pulled out the paper holder. The men recovered somewhat and walked down the hall to the boardroom.

One day at work, I overheard a conversation about herpes. Not knowing what it was, I figured it must be bugs. A month later, a stranger knocked at my apartment door. He spoke with an accent and a lisp. I was shocked as I listened to his sales pitch: he was selling herpes!

When he put his foot in the doorway, I panicked. I told him he shouldn't scare people and suggested that he go to a hospital for treatment. I was under the impression that herpes could jump from one person to another.

He looked surprised and tried to explain that he could show me by putting a sample of his product in my bathtub.

"Go away now or I'll call the police," I screamed.

With a puzzled look on his face, he handed me an envelope. The label read "Natural Herbs."

"Oh, my God, I'm so sorry. Don't expect anyone else to react the way I did." I watched him walk away. When he glanced back at me, I smiled and waved at him, hoping I hadn't traumatized his sales career.

Chapter 34
A Free Trip

Timmy often came over to check up on me. One evening, he recognized the despair in my voice. "Stop worrying about Sam. He'll come home eventually. Here's a Valium. It'll calm you down."

I swallowed it, then sat on a chair facing him and his girlfriend. After a while, I began to experience strange feelings. I knew that Timmy had been experiencing with marijuana and LSD. "What did you give me?" I asked him.

"LSD."

I immediately tried to make myself vomit, but it didn't work. I was so angry with Timmy, but he reassured me that everything would be all right.

I stared at Timmy's girlfriend and was amazed at the weight she had gained in only minutes. "You're too big for my sofa. God, you're so big! Oh my God, you're getting bigger! My sofa, I can't see my sofa anymore!" I panicked when Timmy's head grew huge and his voice echoed in the distance. He must have been somewhat concerned about my behavior because he turned on the radio, hoping it would relax me.

A soft ballad by The Moody Blues was playing. As I leaned over the arm of the sofa and drifted into "Nights in White Satin," a strange calm flowed through me. I hummed along to the song and was astounded that the group had accepted me as a member of their band.

I don't know how long I had entertained Timmy and his girlfriend but, at one point, I snapped out of my delusion. I was alone.

I went to the washroom, stared at the mirror, and took a trip behind my eyes. I was so intrigued by the blood vessels, nerves, and color in my eyes that I let myself investigate deeper. I don't know how long I stood there, but I finally detached myself from the mirror, only to face another dilemma.

The washroom door was locked and I was up to my waist in blood. The room began to fill with thick smog. Breathing became difficult, and I was about to faint when the door miraculously opened, letting the blood surge all over the kitchen floor. I put one foot ahead of the other and waded through the red river.

It seemed like hours before I could sit down again. The blood had vanished and the air was clear. My senses were back but not for long.

A knock at the door propelled me into another nightmare. It was the lady next door. Her teeth were as large as Nellie's and her laugh was a whiney, loud and clear. I gasped in fright.

"What's wrong?" a voice echoed.

She looked so weird that I couldn't stop staring at her. I didn't think horses could talk. I focused on reality long enough to invite her in. She was carrying two fudge ice cream cones and a plate of fish she had cooked for me. Without thinking, I put the fish in a kitchen cabinet instead of the fridge. Food was the last thing on my mind, but I managed to tell her I appreciated the gesture.

As she licked her cone, I watched in awe. Her tongue was thick and long, and it twirled round and round, collecting layers of ice cream that dripped down the sides of her cone. I was sure Nellie was sitting at the table because animated slides of the horse, interspersed by moments of reality, kept flashing alternately before me. The more I tried to figure out one scenario, the faster another one would take over.

There was only one way to avoid further embarrassment: I told my neighbor that I wasn't feeling well and asked her to go home. As she was leaving, she suggested that maybe I was hungry and should eat the fish she had brought.

Later I opened the kitchen cabinet to get a glass but immediately slammed it shut. The fish had turned into crabs and they were crawling all over my dishes. To prevent them from getting out, I tied an elastic band around a pair of door handles.

Overcome by a thirst that meant life or death, I hooked my mouth to the kitchen faucet and drank for the longest time. I sat down, not knowing what to expect next. The apartment was quiet, the children were sleeping, and my mind drifted to places unknown.

All of a sudden, Daniel was standing in front of me. He told me he couldn't sleep. He was so tiny that I asked him to put on a sweater so I could see him. He did. I repeated my request three times. Daniel stood before me, smiling and dressed for a cold winter's day. It was so ridiculous that I laughed along with him, then sent him off to bed. He was quite obedient—a blessing on that unforgettable day.

I was alone again, enjoying a silent moment, when I felt a little head lean against my lap. It was Charlie. I stroked his head while I hummed an unfamiliar song and told him how much I loved him. When he looked up at me, he smiled and one of his beautiful brown eyes popped out of his face and onto my forehead.

I gasped. Then it happened again, yet logic told me it was impossible. I asked Charlie not to look at me to see what would happen, but he found it all so funny that he kept on laughing and staring at me as his eye hit my forehead, over and over again. The next thing I recalled was tucking him in bed and humming a tune I had never heard before.

My situation wasn't improving, so I considered going to the hospital emergency. Maybe they could give me a needle or something to get me over the effects of the LSD. I didn't like the control the drug had over me. I felt too vulnerable.

I was standing on the back porch of my second-floor apartment when I caught a glimpse of paradise. A beautiful creek flowed across the yard, its short silver-tipped waves rippling across transparent water. The sides of the creek were trimmed in gold. It was the perfect place to take a bath and relax.

But how would I get down there? I looked around and didn't see any stairs. I was stuck on the second floor. I considered taking a giant leap and was debating how I'd do it when Charlie interrupted me. Back inside I went, cuddling him in my arms as I hummed another unfamiliar melody until he fell asleep.

Incredible thoughts bounced back and forth in my mind like ping-pong balls and were scaring me to death. My greatest fear was that the house would catch on fire. How would I save the children? My ears were astute to the noises around me, which only intensified my anxiety. I sat on the kitchen floor and guarded the back door as if I were expecting someone. Would I dare to ask God for another favor?

Then it happened. In the doorway stood a glowing figure dressed in white. "Oh my God, is that you?" I asked.

He spoke one word and shattered my illusion. Timmy had felt guilty for having left me alone and had returned to check up on me. I broke into tears. I grabbed onto him and begged him not to leave me alone. He calmed me down and suggested that I try to sleep it off, then left to join his friends.

Moments seemed like hours, and hours seemed like seconds, or time just stood still. I walked toward the bedroom and froze when I saw Sam at the door. He didn't comment on my abnormal behavior. Maybe he didn't notice. I knew he wanted to have sex, but all I wanted was to think clearly. Without saying a word, I went to bed—fully dressed.

Sam undressed and lay on the bed. I felt his hands on me. I took one look at him and started hyperventilating at the sight of his penis. "What the heck is that?" I screamed. I jumped out of bed and ran to the back porch. "He won't come near me with a penis that size!" I said, trembling. I waited until Sam had fallen asleep, then I crawled into bed beside him and dozed off without a problem.

The next morning, flashbacks interrupted my thoughts. I was still confused about what had happened the night before. I poured coffee into a cup and stepped out onto the back porch to get some fresh air. I glanced down at the glittering water that had beckoned me to go for a swim last evening. I shuddered. In its place was a raw sewage creek that flowed along the edge of the property. When I noticed that someone had removed the staircase last night, a wave of relief swept over me.

I wasn't enthused about going to work the next morning. I applied blush to my cheeks to camouflage my tired look. When I leaned over to kiss Sam goodbye, he grabbed me by the hair and smeared my face with the newspaper he was reading. "You know I don't want you to wear makeup," he yelled.

After I washed my face, my cheeks were pink with

humiliation and anger. I kissed Sam goodbye and went to work.

That evening after dinner, Sam went to the corner store for cigarettes and returned three days later with none. I handed him the cigarette rolled at both ends that I had found in his shirt. He smiled as he took it, aware that I had no idea it was marijuana. He smoked it and left the house, leaving me alone again.

"I can't go on like this," I murmured to myself. "How long will he be away this time?"

Another three days passed and Sam hadn't returned, but his hourly calls during the night were driving me to the breaking point. I was standing at the kitchen sink, washing a butcher knife, when Sam opened the door. He sensed that something was wrong and asked, "Can I come in?"

"Please don't move," I replied, the knife still in my hand.

I detected a tinge of fear in Sam's eyes and we both knew something was terribly wrong. He spun around, raced down the stairs, and fumbled on a step as the butcher knife flew by his head.

A repetition of three nights spent answering his hourly calls drained the last bit of energy from me. When Sam eventually came home, he walked into the boys' bedroom and shut the door. I had a master key and locked him in. I took three days off work and, every hour on the hour, I played with the door handle to keep him awake. I had suffered the effects of sleepless nights and he would experience what it felt like.

Three days later, I opened the door. Went to hell and back would appropriately describe his appearance. Lucky for him, some empty pop bottles in the room had served a purpose during his period of confinement.

Sam showered and went to bed. Strange, but I wasn't feeling as powerful as I had expected. Instead I felt regret as the Golden Rule crossed my mind: Do unto others as you would have them do unto you.

Chapter 35
Hide and Seek

When Nanette and her husband moved to California, I lost my rock of support. I realized too late how much my older sister had meant to me. Nanette was a mentor to me and our siblings and the link that kept us above water. The responsibility of having been like a parent to us was bestowed upon her at a young age, yet she carried her love for us deep in her heart.

Nanette gave birth to two daughters and had settled into a comfortable routine, but her concerns for Mom and Dad and the increasing number of long-distance calls prompted her to move back to Canada. Unfortunately, she chose to live four hundred miles away from us.

Mom called me with news that she and Dad were moving to Nanette's hometown. Nanette had arranged for our parents to live in a guest suite attached to her home. My sister was delighted to have Mom live closer to her. She told me she hoped that their proximity to her would limit Dad in expressing his rage toward Mom.

I was happy for Mom but wondered how I'd ever manage without her. I hugged her and said, "I wish I could go with you."

A few days later, Mom called and told me she was going to do something for the children and me that she thought she'd never do: help me to get a divorce. As a fervent Catholic, she was aware that divorce went against the religious teachings of "honor and obey" and "till death do us part." But the idea of moving away and leaving me alone to fight my own battles troubled her immensely, so she gave in. "I already met with a lawyer. I'm going to pay for your divorce."

I was stunned. Did I hear right? Would I be able to leave Sam legally? I was filled with mixed emotions and cried for the longest time. What would I do without him? What would the children think? Should I or shouldn't I? I had a decision to make, but I was afraid to make the wrong one.

The next day, the lawyer phoned me and set up a meeting in his office. I was uneasy as I sat across the desk from him. Although he was polite and pleasant, my trust in men was practically non-existent at this point. The purpose of my visit didn't help matters either.

After the lawyer explained the legal procedures that would be involved, he asked me to think it over. "If you agree to go ahead with the divorce, make an appointment with my secretary, and I'll see you in one week." He shook my hand firmly and I knew I'd be back.

After work that day, I stopped at the clinic for treatment of my varicose veins. Sam was drinking when I arrived home. He noticed the band-aids on my legs and ridiculed me. "You think it will make any difference, that it will make you more attractive? Nothing can help you." He laughed out loud.

Confident that my mother was backing me up and that I'd see the lawyer in a week, I turned to him and told him to shut up or I'd leave.

For whatever reason, he found my words hilarious. He laughed louder and yelled, "Where the hell do you think you'd go? No one would want you. Now make my dinner."

I hesitated, wondering what to do next.

Sam must have sensed my fear and confusion. He snapped his fingers. "Just shut up and make my dinner."

I slowly reached for my purse and walked toward the door. Because Sam couldn't imagine I'd ever leave him, he began to laugh hysterically. Little did he know how serious my intentions were. No insults or threats would make me change my mind this time.

I stayed over at a friend's place that night. The next morning, Sam sent the children to school, but I made certain they never returned home. I called the school principal and asked him to send them to my friend's place instead. It broke my heart when I saw them marching home like little soldiers, doing exactly as they had been told. Then again, it was the only way to ensure that Sam couldn't use them as leverage to draw me back home. Later that day, I went to the lawyer's office and filed for divorce. There was no turning back.

A game of hide-and-seek began. I was hiding and Sam was seeking. He made the first of his visits that night to Mary's home a few doors down the road. She denied having seen us. We held our breaths as the six of us hid in the bedroom.

The next evening, Mary tried to convince me to stay one more night, but I sensed that something bad was going to happen. "No, we must leave right now. Thank you for your help. I'll call you." I rushed out the door with the children and drove to my friend Lorna's home where we spent the night.

Fifteen minutes after I had left Mary's place, Sam came looking for us and ransacked her house. He insisted that she tell him where I was and jabbed his finger into her forehead with every word he said.

The same scene played out over the next two weeks. Either I had left a friend's home just before Sam arrived, or I had arrived right after his angry visit. The children never complained or asked questions. They just puttered along as if they were attached to me with invisible strings.

Sam's arrival at my friends' homes was unwelcome and stressful. He threatened them and swore that when he'd find me, he'd kill me. On one specific occasion, he barged into a friend's house as my children and I huddled at the back of a deep closet. He called the children by name, hoping that they'd surface. He finally left and we were safe for one more night.

During that same two-week period, I traveled to and from work with James, a co-worker at the mining company. He was a short, quiet man with beautiful green eyes, and was so shy that our conversations were limited to good morning and good-bye. He picked me up at a different address every morning and dropped me off at another one after work.

Every morning and late afternoon, Sam parked his car near the entrance to the office building in the hope he'd see me. James parked his car and went in to work, but I crouched on the floor of the car until Sam would leave. James and other employees took turns watching Sam's car. After he drove away and the coast was clear, someone would come and get me. Seeing Sam face-to-face was the only thing that could make me change my mind and stop the divorce proceedings, and I was glad it never happened.

One weekend, James came to see me at a friend's place. "I'm going to the beach. Do you want to come?"

"I'm sorry, James, I can't. But I'll go see you as a butterfly." I laughed and walked him to the car. All of a sudden, I spotted a four-leaf clover. I handed it to him.

He accepted it and smiled.

On Monday, James picked me up for work. He chuckled as I slid in next to him. "You freaked me out. Saturday at the beach, a monarch butterfly hung around me all day." He smiled. "Was that you?"

"Yeah, it was."

#

Sam was furious when he was served with divorce papers. My daring move made him even more determined to find me.

My uncle drove me to the divorce court in a town sixty miles away—the same town where Matthew had been born. I listened as the judge and lawyer exchanged their legal jargon.

The judge wasn't impressed with the amount of one dollar for child support that I had insisted my lawyer record on the divorce papers. "Is this a joke?" he asked me.

"No, it's not a joke," I answered. "The reason for the dollar is to satisfy bureaucracy. I'm not here to cripple Sam."

The judge realized that I was serious. "Divorce granted," he said and hit the desk with his gavel.

My lawyer tapped me on the shoulder and said. "You're a free woman. You can go now."

"But where the hell will I go?"

"Is it possible for you to leave town? Sam is like a lion in a cage and you don't want to open the door."

He was right. I had to do something and soon.

He handed me documents and said, "Here's your copy. You'll receive the official papers in three months."

My uncle walked me to his car. It was parked behind the courtroom out of Sam's view. As we drove off, I felt relief, yet a part of me still wanted to be with Sam. Why hadn't he come to defend himself?

#

Sam was living with his mother. A few days later, I called him and suggested we go over the divorce papers. He agreed to meet with me at my aunt's place. When he walked in, I began to tremble. I was leaving the man I loved, and emotions were interfering with the logic of my decision. We sat at the table and stared at each other, speechless for a few moments before we began to discuss the conditions of the divorce. All the while, our five children sat quietly by and listened.

With sadness in his voice, Sam said, "You have all the children. What should I do?"

"We don't have to follow the irrevocable conditions of the divorce," I replied. "We could share the children, if you want…whenever you want. No one needs to be hurt any more than they already are, Sam."

Matthew, our eldest son, looked at his father and asked if he could stay with him. I left Matthew with Sam the next day. Things turned out better than I expected, but I was unaware that it was the calm before the storm.

With no other place to go to, I returned to the house I had left weeks earlier. Sam was no longer living there. I figured the children and I would be fine for one night. I'd think about my plans for the future tomorrow.

Just before I went to bed, Tina, my friend Mary's eighteen-year-old daughter, called me. She had had an argument with her mother and asked if she could sleep over at my place. I welcomed the thought of having someone stay with me and said yes.

A thousand thoughts flitted through my mind as I lay in bed. I was desperate and certainly couldn't leave town with five children, so I made a decision. I had heard of a woman who lived in the country and babysat children. It would be the best place for the boys.

At two in the morning, Sam banged at the front door. He said he wanted to give the boys a dog. I disregarded the restraining order and let him in. It felt as if a wave hit me as Sam stormed in holding a young Dalmatian in his arms. The anger in his eyes was the worst I had ever seen. It didn't surprise me. Our divorce was official but nothing would stop Sam from being suspicious. Without a word, he charged from room to room, as if he were looking for someone. I was surprised to see that Tina was gone, but I didn't mention it.

The children, wide-eyed and trembling, stood in the stairway and watched their father as he chased me around the house. I avoided Sam's blows, but when a chair hit me across the back, I fell to the floor. I stretched out my arm to grab the phone, but Sam pulled the cord from the wall. I managed to get to my feet when a chair hit me across the neck, and I fell down again.

Sam turned the house upside down in his persistent search for whoever he imagined was hiding there. He went into the washroom, pulled the wringer out of the washing machine, and flung it across the room. He yanked the sewing machine out of its table and hurled it through a wall. He was angrier and stronger than I had ever seen him, so I kept out of his path. He whizzed past me, holding a pair of my panties he had taken from the laundry basket. On his way up the stairs, he passed the children and released his rage by punching holes in the wall.

I was so stunned by what was happening that I barely heard the knock at the front door. I ran to open it. Two police officers stood in the doorway. Tina, alarmed by the shouting, had crawled out the window to a neighbor's home and called the police.

I breathed a sigh of relief. One of the officers asked what the problem was. Just as I opened my mouth to speak, Sam wrapped his arms around me. "We had a party, she's drunk, and we'll quiet down," he said and shut the door in their faces.

"I have divorce papers," I shouted, but Sam muffled my words with his hands. I yanked my arm out of his grip and ran to the living room. I avoided the furniture that swung past me, but a slap threw me into a spin, and I knocked my head against the wall. "Oh, my God!" I screamed.

Sam stopped at the sound of knocking at the front door. His stepfather, who had been waiting in the car, had heard screams coming from the house and decided to check up on Sam. He walked in and looked around in disbelief. He grabbed Sam's arm and insisted he leave with him.

Sam seemed disoriented as his stepfather led him away. But once he reached the door, he turned and pointed at me. "No woman leaves me." He took a deep breath. "No other man will ever touch you, do you understand?"

"I understand what you're saying, Sam," I replied. "Watch me. I'll be the first woman in your family to leave her husband." After I shut the door, I peeked through the curtains. His stepfather was still trying to deter Sam from coming back to finish what he had started. Sam finally opened the car door and got in. His mother and mistress were sitting in the back seat.

Soon after they left, two police officers knocked at the door. They told me they had parked in the back alley and had been waiting for Sam and me to settle our differences. They asked me if I wanted to press charges.

Astonished at their insensitive behavior, I pointed to the damage and said. "If I were to press charges, it would be against you." I slammed the door in their faces.

Early the next day, my parents came over with news. My lawyer had heard about Sam's disruptive visit and had called them to pass along a message to me. Concerned about my safety, my lawyer had suggested that I leave town.

"But where am I supposed to go?" I stared at my parents.

Dad handed me some money. "As far as you can."

Chapter 36
The Escape

James gave me a ride to work the next morning. He mentioned that Tina had called him last night to tell him about the commotion at my house.

I burst out crying and related my version of Sam's horrifying visit. I also told him I had to quit my job and leave town right away.

As James walked with me to the manager's office, he said, "I have to quit my job, too."

"Why would you do that?" I asked.

"I know that you want to leave. I'll bring you wherever you want to go."

Our employer was surprised by our decision to leave the company but understood the seriousness of the situation. He didn't insist on the usual two weeks' notice but kindly arranged for our paychecks and final papers to be ready by noon that same day.

I went through the rest of the afternoon as if I were in a daze. James and I rushed back to the house to pick up a few things and then brought the boys and their belongings to the country. I sobbed as I hugged my children and we said our goodbyes. "I'll come to get you very soon," I promised them.

Matthew's big brown eyes filled with tears. He was hanging onto the Dalmatian. He told me he was fine and all he wanted for the time being was his dog. He walked away from me, probably too overwhelmed by what was going on.

That night, Katie, James, and I slept in the car. In the wee hours of the morning, we were on our way to nowhere. Was I actually leaving? My thoughts weren't clear, but I knew I wanted to go as far away as possible—maybe even as far as British Columbia.

I called my sister Nanette to tell her of my plans. We agreed that I'd call her every other day to get an update on the situation back home.

As James drove, I said nothing and just stared out the car window at the scenery along the highway, not actually seeing the view. Even Katie sat quietly throughout the trip. After driving for hours, we stopped at a campsite and set up tent. We drifted into a restless sleep, only to continue our escape at dawn.

Two days later, I called Nanette. The news was uneventful, which alleviated a bit of stress as we drove on, but my next call to her drained every ounce of hope from my body. The lawyer had a message for me: I must come home immediately or I would lose the boys.

James offered to drive me back to my hometown, but I refused. I didn't want to risk a confrontation between him and Sam. Seeing as we had traveled quite a distance and weren't far from Nanette's hometown, I took Katie and caught the next bus there.

My sister filled me in on what had happened. It seemed that Sam had been driving around and had spotted Matthew riding a bike into town. After Matthew had revealed where the boys were staying, Sam had taken the children and brought them to his mother's apartment.

To my surprise, Dad offered to drive me back home—four hundred miles away—so I could pick up the children. I had never had as much pride and respect for Dad as I did at that moment. He didn't have to give me a reason for his kind gesture. Even though it was no secret how much he disliked Sam and how he would have done anything to put distance between Sam and me, I knew Dad was concerned about my welfare. I couldn't feel safer than with him.

When I arrived in my hometown, I went straight to the police station and asked for an escort to my mother-in-law's apartment.

When Sam opened the door and saw the police officer, he told him to leave. "I don't need your help," he told the officer who had been a personal friend of his for years.

I glanced inside where Sam's girlfriend and his mother were sitting. I could see the hatred in their eyes. In contrast, the stepfather's expression was one of concern.

The officer stood his ground and refused to leave until Sam handed the children over to me. Tense moments followed as the two men exchanged loud and crude words. I finally left with four of my children; Matthew wanted to stay with his father.

Dad drove us back to Nanette's. As arranged, James met us there later that day. He stayed in a trailer parked in Nanette's driveway until we rented a furnished two-bedroom apartment a week later. The three boys slept in bunk beds, Katie slept with me, and James slept on the sofa. Even though we decided to live as a family, the sleeping arrangements remained the same.

In spite of the problems I had endured, I still had faith in the future. Maybe a better life was in store for me…maybe I'd be safe now…maybe I could provide stability for the children…just maybe, I wished, as sleep snuck its way into my worries.

While James was at work one night, the phone rang. A late call always threw me into panic mode. "Hello," I answered. No one spoke, but I knew someone was there because I could hear heavy breathing.

Then Sam spoke. "I'm at the bar at the corner of your street. I'll be over in a few minutes. My warning about another man touching you is still in effect." He hung up.

I felt as if the little valves in my body were closing down, one after the other, shutting the flow of blood and air, and numbing every muscle and nerve. The closet seemed to be the best place to hide, so I gathered the children and we huddled there in the quiet darkness. Even our breathing was soundless.

It seemed as if we had been hiding for the longest time when the phone rang again. I crawled to it on my hands and knees in case Sam might be peeking through the window. Again, no one spoke at the other end of the line. I strained my ear to try to hear the smallest sound.

"Were you scared?" Sam laughed. "I'm not at the corner, but it's only a four-hour drive. You'll never know when I'll be watching you." The phone went dead.

Chapter 37
It's not Over Till It's Over

My parents' lives hadn't changed much, except that they hid their misery better because they lived so close to Nanette. Mom's osteoporosis was quite advanced. Anyone else might have pitied her, but it didn't deter Dad from physically abusing her. They spent their evenings choosing from a variety of pills and liquor, which helped them make it through another night.

Mom still worked as a teacher but she wasn't herself. Smiles were rare and conversations even rarer. Although she was alone in the house with Dad, she frequently had visions and conversations with my children and me. She anchored herself to my family in order to deal with her loss.

Dad called me six months after Sissy's death. I was living in Ottawa at the time. He urged me to come home because Mom was acting strange. When I entered the house, she wasn't surprised to see me since, in her mind, she had seen me every day since my sister's death. She eventually returned to reality but was knocked down a second time by Billy's death. Dad drank even more, if that was possible, and seemed to cocoon himself most of the time in a solitary world of guilt and remorse.

Their health eventually deteriorated to such an extent that they were obliged to go their separate ways. Mom headed for a hospital and Dad, for an old age home. We watched them walk away from their home with a few personal belongings in hand, heading toward a dismal future and leaving nothing but bad memories behind.

Dad had sclerosis of the liver and was dying. I entered his

hospital room one day to find him pale, helpless, and unable to speak. He seemed so small and defenseless in that big bed that my heart went out to him. "Dad, if I've ever done anything in my life to hurt you," I said, "I'm truly sorry. Please forgive me." I planted a kiss on his bald head. "You're my father, and I love you." I held his hand and tried not to cry.

Dad's life had been one of pain and, like a faithful warrior, he had diligently inflicted pain on anyone who crossed his path. His dark blue eyes, now softened by the suffering that accompanied his illness, were not as mean as I had remembered. He probably knew he was dying and was relieved that his agony would soon be over. Even though he believed that no man should ever cry, he had often cried—but only when he was alone. I watched as a tear made its way down his cheek, a tear that Dad was too weak to hold back. That single tear washed away all my anger and I forgave him. He died shortly afterward, and I was confused because I couldn't understand why I felt so sad about his passing.

Dad had made me promise to have him cremated. At the time of his request, I was praying that he would die and thought that his burial day couldn't come soon enough. After his death, I desperately tried to meet his last wish, but I couldn't because I had no say. Everyone else seemed eager to get it over with, so Dad wasn't cremated.

After the funeral services, we were preparing for the drive to the cemetery when the hearse broke down. The drivers were unable to fix it, so they requested another one. We were on our way when the second hearse stopped in its tracks. My heart pounded with guilt. I was sorry that I had failed to convince the others of Dad's request to be cremated.

All of a sudden, the priest blurted out, "You're just as hardheaded—even after death," for he was also aware of my father's last wish.

The guilt lingered inside me for years—until the night I had a vivid dream. I was standing in a funeral parlor, facing a huge glass wall and staring at a coffin that was floating in midair. A silhouette walked into the room and set fire to the coffin. The bottom of the coffin was completely burnt and a body fell to the ground. I froze when I saw it was Dad's. I couldn't understand what was happening.

Dad turned his head and looked at me with those beautiful blue eyes. He winked at me and I woke up. I was cold but then felt warmth around me and realized everything was fine. I no longer felt guilty and I never dreamed of my father again. Thank you, Dad.

Chapter 38
Gifts and Guns

The apartment owners were an odd couple in the sense that the man was hard-working, but Linda, his wife, had a look of malice or mischief about her—or something I couldn't quite put my finger on.

A few days before Christmas, Linda insisted that I go shopping with her. Thrilled that I'd get to shop in the big name stores and buy gifts for the children, I agreed. By the end of our shopping spree, I had a bag filled with inexpensive presents. I couldn't stop chatting about everything I had seen.

But Linda wasn't as enthusiastic. She stopped the car in front of a huge apartment building.

"Why are you parking here?" I asked.

She hesitated. "It's okay. I'm just picking something up at a friend's place." She suggested that I go inside with her. We took the elevator to the fourth floor, walked down a dark hallway, and stopped in front of an apartment door. Linda knocked three times, pausing between each knock.

How strange, I thought. Was it some kind of code?

The door opened to reveal a tall man in his thirties: sandy-blond curly hair, green eyes, a plaid shirt unbuttoned halfway down, and jeans. He was barefoot and hadn't shaved for a day or so, but it didn't take away from his rugged good looks. Linda hugged him and then introduced me to Rex. The tone of his voice and the way he spoke told me he was in charge.

The living room had no furniture, except for a couch and a wood box. Linda and Rex sat down on the couch, but I stayed by the door. Rex kept staring at me while he and Linda spoke in hushed voices. I felt as if I were on display, but for what? During the next half hour, the two of them exchanged French kisses and intimate touching. I begged Linda to drive me home, but she ignored my pleas.

I was still standing by the door, shopping bags in hand and ready to run, when I heard the key turn in the lock. As a short scrawny man stepped inside, I caught a whiff of him and wanted to gag. He wore a baseball cap, a dark blue shirt that hung loosely over hunched shoulders, and a pair of pants two sizes too large for him. He studied me from head to toe, then his lips parted to reveal rotten teeth. He glanced at Rex and nodded yes. Fearing the worst, I insisted that Linda take me home right away.

Rex frowned. He grabbed Linda's arm and whispered in her ear, then he pushed her away. She pouted as the grubby little man escorted her down the hallway to another room.

Rex asked me my name, took me by the hand, and told me not to be afraid of him. He led me into a room that had no furniture except for a bed. He ordered me to sit and I did. I felt helpless, as if I were entangled in a tight rubber band with no one around to free me. Rex wasn't talking, only staring, so I stared back. Something told me we weren't thinking about the same thing.

"I'm going to sit next to you," Rex said and slowly approached.

The minute he sat on the bed, I stood up against the wall.

He seemed confused. He ordered me to sit down again and, without taking his eyes off me, he leaned into the closet and picked up a rifle. After he cocked it, he pointed it straight at my head. He stared at me as if he were searching for something. He lowered the rifle and pointed it at my chest. Without saying a word, he put the rifle back in the closet and took out a pistol. He pointed it at my head. "Do you know what the Mafia is?" His voice had a serious tone to it.

I nodded yes. "Al Capone?" was all I could think of.

"I always get what I want. This is the first time I do something so stupid," he said in anger.

I was so petrified that I couldn't move. Tears rolled down my face.

Rex seemed to awaken from a trance and looked away. He

turned back to me and said, "Please don't be afraid. I won't hurt you."

He held me tightly in his arms for a few moments, then held me inches away. "I don't know why I'm letting you go." He paused and looked intensely at me. "I never let a woman go without having had sex with her."

I jumped into his arms. "Thank you, thank you so much."

"Please don't tell Linda what happened. Do we have a deal?"

"Anything you say." I crossed my heart and spit on the floor twice to convince him.

"I don't want you hanging around with Linda. Do you understand? Promise me."

"Yes, I understand. I promise."

"You could get into serious trouble." Rex hugged me again. "I'm sorry." He walked me to the door, put my shopping bags in my hand, and headed toward the second bedroom.

Was I dreaming? Was this man really letting me go?

Harsh words echoed from the bedroom, but it was clear that Rex had won the argument. Moments later, a half-dressed Linda was pushed into the living room.

"I'll talk to you later," Rex shouted as he pointed a finger at her.

Neither Linda nor I spoke during the drive back home.

I sat up all night, thinking about what had happened in Rex's apartment. It was difficult to deal with his unexpected apology and his warning about Linda, let alone his collection of guns.

Early the next day, Linda's daughter came to get me. There was a phone call for me on their phone. "Hi, it's Rex. Did you make it home all right? Are you okay?"

"Yes, I'm fine, thank you."

"Listen, you're not the kind of woman to hang around with Linda. I just want to make sure you understand."

"I do. It'll never happen again."

"Remember our agreement?"

"I remember." I couldn't believe this was the same man that had chilled my blood just yesterday. "I can't thank you enough," I said.

Rex laughed. "You have beautiful eyes. Take care."

I told him he was a gentleman and thanked him again before hanging up. Then I thanked God for having saved me from a situation that could easily have gone from bad to worse.

Chapter 39
Gifts of Appreciation

Mom's health was improving, so we made plans for her to leave the hospital and live at the priest's house. She agreed because she felt she'd be closer to God there. She was sixty-nine and a widow when Hugh, the prospector boyfriend she had dated fifty years ago, came back into her life. They dated a few times and discovered they were still in love. He loved her as much as he did when she was nineteen and, as the song goes, he only had eyes for her.

When Mom had left him to marry Dad, Hugh had told her that he would love only one woman and that he'd wait for her. Fifty years later, they were married. The last picture in Hugh's photo album was one of him skiing with Mom when she was nineteen. The next picture he put into his album was one of the happy couple taken at their wedding.

Throughout the years that Hugh had waited for Mom, he had taken to the bottle to try to forget his loss and had inevitably become an alcoholic. But it hadn't mattered in the end. Being married to Mom was his dream come true. To Hugh, her wheelchair was invisible. He walked with her every day, pushed the wheelchair with one hand, and held her hand with the other. It was as if he were afraid he'd lose her again.

A trip to Florida became a yearly excursion and helped them to avoid the cold Canadian winters. On their fourth annual vacation there, Hugh went for a swim but immediately came out of the water. He had experienced tightness in his chest. He tried to swim a few more times but felt the same discomfort in his chest, so he decided to go shopping alone instead. He bought Mom a pretty dress and a beaded necklace.

They sat at the dinner table that evening, gazing into each other's eyes. Hugh expressed his love for Mom and told her how beautiful she looked in the outfit he had purchased. He leaned back in his chair to admire her, then crunched over and fell to the ground. He died instantly of a heart attack.

Mom couldn't accept the fact that Hugh was gone. Now and then, I'd bring up the subject and tell her that she was a very lucky woman. She did have four wonderful years with him and should be thankful. She'd nod and smile, but I could tell that she was heartbroken.

We often talked about her love for Hugh and the reason she left him for Dad. Dad was a stranger. He was handsome and intriguing. Other women wished he would ask them out, but Mom was the chosen one.

"That's all in the past," she'd say with a wistful sigh.

One thing that never changed was Mom's requests for favors from saints that she constantly prayed to. Once I walked into her room and noticed that a statue had been turned around. "Mom, why is St. Jude facing the wall again?"

"I'll turn him around when he gives me what I asked for." She gave me a sly smile that meant "and you can bet I'll get it."

#

James was as respectable a family man as he could be. I often watched him as he took on the role of protector and provider to the children and me.

As we sat talking one evening, it dawned on me that he had given up his life to help me and had never asked for anything in return. I wanted to repay him somehow and came up with the perfect gift. James was speechless when I offered him a gift that had no price tag: a baby. Our relationship soon became more intimate. The day I told him I was pregnant, his face lit up with joy and gratitude. His appreciation meant the world to me.

It was mid-October. I was three months pregnant when I decided I wanted to move again. I called my brother Timmy who lived about eight hundred miles further north where jobs in the mining industry were plentiful. Anticipating similar weather in that part of the country, I packed our belongings accordingly. I couldn't believe my eyes when we arrived there. It was a frosty forty degrees below zero with snow piled up to five feet high in some areas.

I met with the manager of a gold mine, told him I was a paymaster, and asked for a job. He hired me on the spot. Then I asked that he hire James too.

James and I worked the same hours, so once again he was my driver. I stared out the window on our first trip to work together. This time, I gazed at the beautiful scenery and took the time to admire it.

Since James had to work overtime one day, a co-worker offered to drive me home. Not feeling at ease in the man's presence, I refused and waited for four hours until James finished his shift. The next day, I found out that he had raped a girl who had accepted his offer to drive her home. I thanked God that I had made the right choice.

It was two weeks past my due date, and I was having contractions. I left a note on the kitchen table to tell James that I had gone to the hospital.

The hospital attendants wheeled me to the delivery room. When the doctor walked in, I flew into a panic. He had dark skin, black hair, and dark piercing eyes. I screamed and yelled for someone to help me and protect me from the doctor. He pulled off his surgical mask and I instantly calmed down. It wasn't Sam.

The doctor asked me how many children I had and what I'd like this time.

"I'd like a boy," I replied as though he could order it on request.

The delivery went well and, for the first time, I held my baby after birth. When I had delivered the first five children, I had been put to sleep right after birth and had never had a chance to see the babies until after they had been washed and dressed. Only then did I find out if I had had a boy or a girl. Now I was able to check Jacob's fingers and toes and admire the beauty of my tiny newborn. This was a good thing, I said to myself.

Chapter 40
Please Don't Go

I was home with my baby Jacob when I received a call from Sam. He congratulated me on my recent birth, which came as quite a surprise to me.

Sam seemed more relaxed each time he came over to visit the children. He enjoyed taking them fishing or playing ball with them. In turn, the children looked forward to their happy visits with Sam, and their relationship with their father blossomed in ways I couldn't possibly imagine. Although it wasn't before Katie turned seven that Sam accepted her, the love between them strengthened and they became inseparable.

Oddly enough, I missed the smell of Sam's cologne, and when he smiled at me, I melted. I tried to hide my feelings from him because our lives had taken different paths, but Sam could always see through me. We didn't need words to know how we felt about each other. He still loved me and I still loved him. After all, he had given me a precious gift: our children. Yet even though our love had survived destructive storms and subsequent pain, Sam and I had had to face the unshakable truth that we couldn't live together. The connection between us was still strong, but it would remain a secret, a secret that would allow others around us to be happy and confident and get on with their lives.

My family doctor had once asked me why I was living in the country like a hermit. I had lied and told him I was happy. But when I no longer had a reason to fear Sam, I decided to change residence and move closer to him—especially for the children's sake. I convinced James that we should rent a house about twenty miles away from my hometown.

It was Sam's turn to pick up the children at my home. His girlfriend preferred to wait in the car while Sam had a coffee and enjoyed a bit of arm-wrestling with James. Later, as Sam was preparing to leave, I peeked through the curtains and watched him put the children's belongings in the trunk of the car. He saw me in the window and crouched down so his girlfriend couldn't see him. He waved and sent kisses my way. I think Sam finally felt the same kind of love for me as I had for him.

Christmas was a few days away. I had just finished my shopping when I decided to drop in on Sam where he worked in a men's clothing store. I could tell he was happy to see me. We were talking about the children and our plans for the holidays when I noticed tears welling up in his eyes.

I struggled to contain my feelings and made a move to leave when Sam gently took hold of my arm and said, "Can I kiss you Happy New Year, black beauty?"

My heart was pounding so hard. I was tempted to say yes, but I refused.

"Maybe it's for the best," Sam said. He took a deep breath as he put his hands on each side of my face. "I think if I'd kiss you, I'd die of a heart attack. I love you so much."

After we said our goodbyes, I stood on the sidewalk in front of the store and was overcome with intense emptiness, loneliness, and sadness. I looked up at the starless sky. "I love you too, Sam."

Weeks later, the phone rang as I was starting to fall asleep. I figured whoever it was would call back tomorrow. Early the next morning, the phone rang again. As I listened to the message at the other end of the line, my knees went weak. Sam had died of a heart attack. He hadn't been feeling well and had gone to his mother's home to phone me last night. The fact that I hadn't answered his call caused me deep regret. Sam was gone, and contrary to what anyone else might have expected, turmoil set in for the children and me.

I spent three days at the funeral parlor and couldn't remember much about it, except that people spoke to me in slow, muffled voices. However, I do recall the vast amount of flowers and wreaths they managed to stack into one room. It reminded me how Sam used to joke about his death by saying, " I hope to receive lots of flowers when I die."

"Well, Sam, more than you'll ever know," I whispered.

Sam's coffin was about to be closed and I hadn't paid my final respects yet. Every time I had made an effort to approach the coffin, someone had rushed there ahead of me. After everyone had left the funeral parlor, I was granted a few minutes with Sam so I could say goodbye. His hair felt rough as I passed my hand through it. Sam had never allowed me to touch his hair since he would usually set it in place with hairspray. Now I messed his hair and he didn't react. It felt like a dream as I slowly lifted his head and whispered, "I'm so sorry, Sam. I love you. I wish…I wish." I couldn't say another word. It was time to let go, but how could I?

The rest of the day was a blur, except for what others told me afterward. I couldn't recall the church, the burial, or anything else regarding Sam's funeral. And since then, I've never found the missing pieces to help me put that day in order.

After Sam's death, the children cried every time they reminisced about their father and talked about their pleasant experiences with him. I encouraged this interaction between us because it was the only way they could express their pain. But it became clear to me that the mere mention of Sam's name made James uncomfortable. I made sure the children were aware of James' feelings and told them they could come to me in private whenever they wanted to discuss their father. But there was no more laughter in the house, and the children staggered along with a burden of emptiness too heavy for their tiny hearts to carry.

I became especially worried when Katie began to have fainting spells. She fainted at the table while having breakfast or when I brushed her hair. Because she missed her father very much, she wrote letters to him that I later found hidden under her mattress. One night, I was awakened by whispering. I traced it to Katie's room and found her on her knees holding a picture of Sam. She was crying and wanted him back.

I brought Katie to the family doctor. When I explained what was happening to my children and me, the doctor insisted that I leave James and go back to the city. "You and your children are very unhappy. You need to change your life."

This time I took the doctor's advice. I told James that I had to leave. We agreed that I would take the six children and their clothes—nothing more. We also agreed that I wouldn't ask him for child support for his son Jacob.

James suggested that I reassess my life over the following year. If I decided to go back to him at that point, I was welcome to do so.

I knew I had hurt him, but I had to leave so that the healing could take place. I moved to an apartment in town suitable for the children and me. Because the cemetery was located close to my home, I often found myself sitting on Sam's grave. I'd talk about the day we met, the obstacles we had to surmount, our children, and the powerful love we once had. Because Sam had conditioned me to tell him everything, I continued to do so. At times I felt ashamed and wondered why I still had the need to relate every tiny detail to him. Hours flew by like minutes and, occasionally, I was surprised to see the sun peeking over the horizon. "Time to get ready for work. Bye, Sam," I'd whisper.

I was running through the cemetery on my way home one day and thought I heard the song "Wildflower" by Skylark, as loud and clear as if it were coming from the sky. I supposed that, deep inside, I wanted Sam to let go of the grip he had on me.

Over the next few months, my health deteriorated and I lost a lot of weight. Several tests indicated that I needed a hysterectomy.

I was recovering in the hospital after surgery and was just about to fall asleep when I heard two young voices call out, "Mom!" Eleven-year-old Katie and three-year-old Jacob rushed in and handed me a bouquet of dandelions and weeds interspersed with wild flowers. The bouquet was the most beautiful one I had ever received. The idea that these children had gathered the flowers and walked the lengthy road to my bedside made my heart sing with joy. Their faces glowed with love and fresh tears rolled down their cheeks. The image of Jacob's beautiful green eyes, his little hat sitting crooked on his head, and Katie's blue eyes were subjects worthy of Renoir's canvas. These images, along with many other memories of my children, remain forever vivid in my mind.

Later that afternoon, I had a reaction to a painkiller. I imagined bugs were crawling all over my bed and I hurled myself to the floor. The children didn't understand what was happening but tried to help as their little hands brushed away the imaginary bugs.

I experienced more of these hallucinations and, during one such incident, the doctor walked into my room. "What is all the commotion about?" he asked. After a frustrated nurse explained that she had changed the bed three times, the doctor concluded that I had had an adverse reaction to the medicine. He prescribed a substitute.

In the months that followed, I had to undergo another operation, but it couldn't be performed in town. So I took the bus to Nanette's four hundred miles away and flew back home. My neighbor Pauline and my son Jacob met me at the airport. As I entered the airport lobby, I heard a child cry out, "*Mon amour*! My love!" It was Jacob, arms outstretched as he greeted me again with a few weeds in his hand and tears that parted his long eyelashes into tiny bunches. Jacob will make a fine Romeo for a lucky Juliet one day, I thought.

#

It was Christmas again, but sadness still filled our lives. The tree in the corner of the living room was decorated with a few Christmas balls and six one-dollar bills fastened with clothespins. The children and I sat in front of the tree until midnight, when we hugged one another and sadly drifted back to our rooms. We lay in our beds and filled the air with "I love you's" until the last faint whisper meant everyone had fallen asleep.

Through the years that followed, Christmas was neither a carbon copy of the previous one nor was it a celebration that I anticipated or could easily afford. It was an occasion that brought our family closer. If I could afford inexpensive gifts, it enhanced the occasion. Otherwise, the children and I exchanged personal cards and heart-warming hugs to show our love. Tears of joy flowed freely, if only because we had survived so much and were still together.

Chapter 41
Trust

It was New Year's Eve. Matthew wanted to borrow my car—a car that I had recently purchased with money that Mom had given me. I gazed at the tall, handsome man in front of me and pondered what I should do. He looked much older than seventeen and, even though I had no insurance, I decided it would be all right and handed him the keys.

Matthew promised to call me when he arrived at his destination and again the next morning before leaving. "Don't worry, Mom. I'm staying at my friend's place and I won't be driving the car tonight."

The next morning, I was invited to a friend's place for breakfast. As I was sipping my coffee, I overheard a few words spoken between two friends in the medical profession but paid little attention to the rest of their conversation.

"What do you think?" one of them asked me.

I tried to make sense of the bit I had heard and replied, "I'm petrified of those things. They don't wait until you're dead to attack."

The room fell silent. Several women stared at me in disbelief. One of the doctors began to laugh hysterically. "Don't change, Diane. I like you just the way you are," he said, patting my back. I had no idea what was going on except that he had brought the room back to life, and people began to chat among themselves again.

I didn't want to miss Matthew's call, so I got up to leave. A friend escorted me to the door and said that she had no idea what I was talking about earlier. "Oh well," I said. "It doesn't really matter."

I was relieved when I saw my car in the driveway but shocked when I saw the driver's door ripped from its hinges. I ran into the house, checked every room, and screamed out Matthew's name. I was relieved when I found him sitting on my bed. I didn't scold him but gave him a chance to explain what had happened.

He had driven a woman home because her husband had been too drunk to drive. The night was cold and a thin layer of snow covered the road. On the way back, he hit an icy patch under the snow and slid directly into a parked car. Because Matthew had no driver's license and his friends fled the scene, he drove away.

I went to the police station and took responsibility for the accident. The car that Matthew had hit belonged to my babysitter's brother. The damage was eight hundred dollars. I lost my license for three years. Matthew and I learned a tough lesson that day.

#

Months later, I met one of the women I had had coffee with on New Year's Day. She was still confused about my response to their question and didn't hesitate to ask for an explanation.

I gave her the same answer I had given her the last time we were together. "They're ugly and they peck at animal bodies even though they're still alive."

She stared at me with a blank expression.

"What?" I asked. "What's wrong?"

"What do you mean by that? I don't understand."

"Those birds," I said.

She thought about it, then laughed so hard that bubbles trickled out of her mouth. "Oh, my God! We were talking about condoms, not condors."

At a loss for words, I smiled and hugged her, then said goodbye and went on my way.

Chapter 42
Unconditional Love

Timmy offered me his trailer and charged me no rent. In spite of his generosity, I still had to take on three jobs to make ends meet. I worked five days a week in the accounting department of an automobile firm, five evenings a week in a hotel dining room and bar, and twelve-hour shifts for Tilden at the airport on weekends. I found it hard to unwind after a nineteen-hour day and often fell asleep at the kitchen table, only to get up the next day and start all over again.

After two years of working seven days a week, I fainted while driving home one night and regained consciousness in the hospital. The emergency doctor scolded me when I told him I had three jobs. The Good Samaritan who had brought me to the hospital had seen my car zigzag and come to a stop along the edge of the road. He had initially thought I was under the influence of alcohol but then found me unconscious.

"If you don't quit two of your jobs, you'll be six feet under in a few months," the doctor advised me, lines of concern etched across his forehead.

I swore no man would ever make me cry again, so I blamed my tears on fatigue, even though I knew the doctor was right. I quit the hotel and weekend jobs and set out to put my life in order. But because I had been bossed around and told what to do all my life, I found it difficult to anchor my thoughts and obligations onto a blueprint, let alone follow them.

One day at work, I was chatting with my friend Lynn in the auto parts department when a man caught my attention. Curly brown hair, full lips, and a neatly trimmed beard enhanced his tall frame and broad shoulders. He had a dazzling smile and he seemed to be quite involved in handling inventory paperwork. His name was Andy.

I often made up excuses to leave my desk on the second floor and go downstairs to catch a glimpse of him. I'd experience a butterfly feeling just knowing he was around. Whenever he looked my way and smiled, I blushed.

I was pretending to listen to Lynn's gossip one afternoon on our break, but my eyes wandered around the auto shop. Andy was standing a few feet from me. When he turned and smiled at me, butterflies floated around in my stomach with nowhere to go. I went back to see Lynn almost every day just to sneak a look at Andy and experience the strange but enjoyable feelings inside me.

One evening, Lynn invited me for a drink at a piano bar. I was sipping on a soda pop when Andy walked in. He came up to us and asked, "May I sit at your table?"

As he pulled up a chair next to me, I hoped he wouldn't notice that my legs were shaking. I blushed and felt lightheaded. All of a sudden, the song "Feelings" began to play.

"Dance?" Andy asked me.

As we glided onto the dance floor, he gently took me in his arms. My heart was racing. It took every ounce of my breath to answer questions as simple as, "How are you?" I leaned against him, hoping to mask my nervousness. I felt as if we were the only two people on the floor.

A beautiful relationship began between us. Songs kept me grounded night after night as the radio played some of my favorite songs: "Feelings," "Dream Weaver," "If You Leave Me Now," "You Don't Know Me," and "All By Myself." Andy became my lifeline and a true friend. We chatted, laughed, and joked as we rode around town. Months passed before I accepted the fact that I needed him in my life. Even though he was married and was going through difficult times, I believed our relationship was respectable because we had only kissed.

One evening, Andy parked his car at the entrance to a quaint motel. He looked uncertain as he turned toward me and asked, "Do you think we should get a room?"

"Sure," I said, excited about the idea. I wasn't expecting that we'd do anything other than talk, laugh, and maybe kiss.

An artificial aroma camouflaged the smell of cigarette smoke in the motel room. A large velvet painting hung crooked on the wall over the bed. "What am I doing here?" I wondered.

Andy slipped into the washroom, took a shower, and came out fully dressed and smelling of soap. His dark curly hair was messy, which made him even more attractive. I went next and also came out fully dressed. I felt strange and didn't know what to do. Being alone with Andy excited me and frightened me at the same time. I was afraid he might want to get intimate and that was the last thing I had in mind.

Hours passed as we wrestled, tickled, laughed, and chased each other around the room. All the while, my cardigan had sat on a bedside lamp to dim the light, but now it was smoking and about to catch on fire. As I pulled it off the lamp, I began to feel uneasy about the whole situation. "I think we should go now."

"Okay," Andy said with a smile. He walked toward the door and opened it.

His easygoing attitude melted away my apprehension and I giggled. "I had a great time. We should do this again."

I didn't sleep that night just thinking about how gentle Andy had been with me, even while we were wrestling, and how safe his sincere laughs had made me feel. Our time together reminded me of the secure feeling I used to have when I visited the lumberjacks.

Weeks later, Andy and I returned to the same motel. We showered, wrestled, and laughed. I lay down on the bed, exhausted, arms stretched out, still giggling. Andy bent over and kissed me. To my surprise, I responded. His kiss was soft, yet intense, and went on forever. I enjoyed the feelings I was experiencing and didn't want it to end. What happened next was unexpected—especially since I had assumed that only men could enjoy sex. Without remorse or fear or guilt from sin, I opened my heart to Andy. We made love several times and I did nothing to stop it.

Afterward, we lay side by side on the bed for the longest time. Every touch and every emotion I had just experienced triggered content, relief, and excitement. Andy had given me the gift of love, and I finally understood the meaning of total trust and affection. And I loved him.

I sat in the doctor's office and explained my experience with these newfound feelings. The same doctor that I had called a pig ten years earlier smiled as I chatted away. The smile on his face told me he took pleasure in listening to me as I described every detail. "I'm happy for you," he said.

"What do you mean by that?" I asked. "Is there something wrong with me? Do you have any medicine to cure me?"

"You're a very lucky woman to have met a man like Andy. Many women have had bad experiences and never get to know what making love is."

I thought about a neighbor who couldn't wait for her husband to return from a trip and about Sam's mistress. I wondered if this was what everyone had been talking about. Most of all, I wondered why Sam and I hadn't experienced such feelings. The doctor's response didn't convince me, but I was glad to accept it because making love with Andy had been so special.

Andy and I often returned to the same motel room. My heart skipped a beat and butterflies flew inside me every time we were together. But I had to be realistic about our relationship. Andy's marital problems had driven him in my direction. Both he and his wife had been unfaithful to each other, so one couldn't possible blame the other for the turmoil in their marriage. They were young restless hearts in search of forbidden pleasures.

I didn't doubt that Andy had feelings for me. But he loved his wife, and as much as I cared for him, I was willing to let him go if it was what he needed and wanted. So when Andy came to me for advice, we worked out a plan to help make his marriage work. I pointed out that he and his wife were angry and that they had destroyed their trust in each other, but the damage was reparable. I suggested that Andy treat his wife with kind words and gestures, bring her flowers for no reason, and show her honesty and forgiveness. Taking these steps was of the utmost importance.

Sleepless nights followed. I felt Andy slipping away from me and saw his eagerness to get his marriage back on track. I suspected that we were in the final phase of our relationship. During our last night together, we made love. I couldn't control my pain or hide the tears as he kissed me goodbye.

My world had crumbled again. I had never told Andy how

much I loved him because I sensed that he was determined to make his marriage work. More roadblocks weren't what he needed. I only hoped that I'd find that special feeling again one day.

With Andy's departure, my survival kit had been taken away from me. I filled my days with so many responsibilities that I seldom took the time to consider the only worthwhile aspect that remained in my life—my children. My existence became a blur of mistakes, one after the other. I didn't fit in anywhere on this earth.

Chapter 43
My Last Escape

I had fooled myself into thinking that I had won the battle against pain when, in fact, I was self-destructing at high speed. The saying, "No one can help you but yourself," applied to everyone else but not to me. I made friends with the wind, never dropping anchor as I created storms, shocked those around me, and drowned my emotions; never looking back for fear I might see the destruction of hearts; never looking back so as to avoid reality and its obligations.

My senses were wild and hungry for new experiences, so I did what came naturally: I moved to a different residence in town several times. With no clue about how to change my life for the better, I wandered into relationships that destroyed my self-worth. I couldn't control my quest for revenge, so I gave in to the urge to inflict pain on others. The "Thou Shalt Not" rules that once were so clear in my mind had now become vague and faded. My pain was locked in a cage and my silent cries for help were not heard. Time meant nothing while I wandered about like a lost soul.

A few years later, the wind abandoned me and the storm blew over. A part of me was missing. I couldn't see, hear, or feel. It was like playing the piano with one hand. I needed the other hand, the one I had temporarily lost—the one that my children represented—because music has to be played in harmony. When I grasped the extent of my children's unconditional love and patience as they waited for me to return to them mentally and emotionally, I realized that I had been living with angels. We wouldn't be complete unless we were together.

I had learned my lesson the hard way. The Golden Rule, "Do

unto others as you would have them do unto you," resurfaced. I was happy to back in my children's lives again. From that point on, my children became my priority. Relationships with men were too painful anyway, so I made a point of ending them before they developed into anything more serious.

I had help in trying to put my life back in order. I felt as if a mysterious entity stood constantly by my side–an entity that would in no way let me suffer more than I could endure. Whenever I stumbled and learned my lesson, the entity helped me up, put me on solid ground, and guided me along until the next time.

I began to evaluate my situation and take a closer look at the thoughts that had been embedded in me as a child. They were tarnished, thickened with remorse, and difficult to erase. But I was determined to change. First I had to cut loose from the painful memories that had a grip on my sanity. I needed to become the person that was dying to surface—the real me—before I'd turn into a mold of the previous generation that I so feared would happen—the generation of people who allowed their hurt to sift into innocent minds to ease their own pain. I couldn't—and wouldn't—let it happen to me. I'd cleanse myself of all feelings and memories that had prevented me from becoming the person I wanted to be and kept me from enjoying life and the wonderful things it offered. I decided that, if I changed my thinking, it would change my choices, which would automatically improve my life.

I was aware that forgiving myself for having hurt others wasn't enough. Self-hatred was a powerful, destructive tool that blocked any sincere emotion. While I was in the shower one day, I tried to wash away the negativity, scrubbing my skin until it hurt. I stood in front of the mirror and hated what I saw, but I lingered there anyway and tried to find something—anything—about me that was attractive. But I couldn't because the hatred was so deep inside me.

The idea of moving far away became more and more inviting. I mentioned to a co-worker that I wanted to move to Florida and work there. She suggested we leave together, so I sold all my belongings. My oldest boys had jobs and were living on their own. I asked my son Matthew, who was nineteen years old and working, if he could keep Katie until I returned. Katie was fond of Matthew and I knew she'd be in good hands. I sent Jacob to his father who promised to take care of him until I'd come back. I was determined to make a life for the children and myself. But it didn't work out.

I was exhausted and nothing seemed to make sense. I was a fugitive running from my feelings or any experience that might make me face reality and take on responsibility. In a strange twist of fate, I feared everything that I was desperately craving for.

Six weeks later, I visited Nanette—my pillar and my guide. I admired my sister and the fine-looking family she had with a husband who loved her. I envied her and wondered why she had everything. Had I stayed in one place long enough, I thought, maybe I'd have had it all, too.

I had often dreamed of living in a bachelor apartment, so I rented one. The feeling of a small place added to my sense of security. A hideaway bed, an extra couch, a table, and two chairs were my belongings. My youngest children, Katie and Jacob, were my treasures. A scented candle filled the air with perfume. I finally had a place I could call my home.

As the fear of men surfaced, I backed into my protective cocoon. My belief was that men were like pieces of chicken covered with "Shake-and-Bake." Put them in a bag, shake well, and they all come out looking the same and wanting the same thing. Inside my cocoon, I was safe and no one could touch me.

#

Down to my last dollar, I sat in a dimly lit restaurant, sipping coffee and going over the want ads in a local newspaper. The musty smell of the faded carpets and the morbid red curtains bordering the windows did nothing to alleviate my depressed state of mind.

A waitress came up to my table and asked me if I was looking for a job. Minutes later, I was hired. I rushed back to Nanette's and asked her to make me a black skirt to wear with my white blouse since I was starting my waitress job that same evening.

Within weeks, my life took a turn for the better. I was making enough money to pay the rent and buy a bit of food. I waited on tables, ambling along in my three-inch heels—something I had always wanted to do. I felt tall and in control. It felt great.

But working as a waitress had its frustrating moments. Customers spewed impolite remarks lined with crude innuendos. Men of different ages sat at the same table for hours, night after night, their eyes following my every move. They wore out their bottoms while trying my patience. Their jokes and laughter seemed to be aimed in my direction, or was I just being paranoid?

One day, a blond-haired man walked in. He was shorter than me and had beautiful blue eyes. He looked exhausted and placed his big dirty hands on the table. A coffee was all he wanted. He had an air of sincerity about him that I hadn't noticed in other men in a long time. The next evening, he returned to the restaurant. He had cleaned up his appearance, but he couldn't change the "good-guy" demeanor he had about him. His name was Pierre.

The following day, Pierre came in for a hot chocolate. I was excited when he remembered my name. "You hire tall waitresses, don't you?" he said to my employer.

I took my shoes off and stood in front of him. "I'm not that tall. See?" I lost myself in his blue eyes.

He took two steps back and smiled.

I often glanced out the front window of the restaurant, hoping Pierre would come in for a coffee. He came in almost every night and told me clean jokes that made me laugh so hard, I had to hide in the washroom in case I'd have an accident. It felt good to laugh and I wished I had more customers like Pierre. While another waitress and I were counting our tips one night, I joked that I'd marry Pierre without hesitation. We laughed about it.

Pierre walked in for dinner with a group of people. When it was time to leave, he came up to me and gave me a generous tip. His companions dug out money from their pockets and piled it on the table. I wanted to tell them that Pierre had already left a tip, but he placed a finger vertically over his lips to warn me not to say anything.

The mere likelihood of seeing Pierre made my job more tolerable. One evening, the boss was too busy to drive me home, so he asked Pierre if he would. All of a sudden, other men in the restaurant came forward with their offers to drive me home. I froze, since fear and mistrust still influenced my feelings. On the drive home, I asked Pierre to drop me off a block from where I lived. I later found out that he had waited until I turned on the lights so he could see which apartment I lived in.

Two days later, a snowstorm blasted into town. I was concerned because I had left my apartment windows partly opened.

Several male customers offered to go to my apartment to close the windows, but I wasn't comfortable with their offers and pretended not to hear them. When Pierre walked in, I immediately handed him my keys and asked him if he would please shut the windows in my apartment. I later found out that he had opened my fridge and had found it empty except for one can of milk sitting on a shelf.

The next day, there was a knock at my door. I opened it and almost tripped over four bags of groceries. I was upset that someone had made a mistake with the deliveries. I was moving the bags over to my neighbor's door, when I spotted Pierre peeking around the corner. He carried the bags back to my apartment, explaining how they had fallen off a truck and that he had picked them up.

I didn't believe him but I didn't know what else to do, so I accepted the groceries. I invited him in for coffee and laughed at his jokes. He was the right medicine for me and I didn't feel obliged to give him anything in return.

Pierre often had surprises for me, like the time I found a racing bike outside my door with a note that read: "You don't have to be afraid to walk home anymore." I was thrilled. Now I could avoid walking past a certain hotel that had drunk men loitering in front of it.

On another occasion, Pierre left a tape recorder with a note telling me to press the button, which I did. I listened to his rich, melodious voice singing a song that he had composed just for me. I was convinced that he ranked alongside the best opera singers in the world.

Chapter 44
Wedding Bells

Two years had passed and life was looking good. I had my bachelor apartment, a full-time job, and my dear friend Pierre who often made me laugh to the point of tears.

Mom was living in a home close by. We went to garage sales from time to time and bought trivial items, if only for the fun of it. The first time I went to a garage sale with Pierre, I had been too shy to get out of the car. I had slid down in the seat so no one could see me. When I finally did get the courage to go, I'd give the owners more money than what they asked, assuring them that their selling price wasn't enough.

I examined every corner of my tiny bachelor apartment and decided I wanted to buy a house. I called Nanette who was working as a real estate agent. The first house she showed me had no back yard. The second one was the one I wanted, even though it had more than enough room for just Katie, Jacob, and me.

"What do I have to do to buy this house?" I asked my sister.

After explaining the process, Nanette said she'd lend me the money for the down payment. I could get a grant from the government and pay her back later.

As the owner of my own house, I had moved up another step in life. A young man who lived in the bachelor apartment next to mine had been a victim of thalidomide and worked for the government. When I told him I was moving, I sensed he was sad, so I asked him if he would be interested in renting a room in the basement of my home. He was ecstatic and the rent he offered covered my mortgage payment.

Soon Pierre was at my front door with a second-hand fridge and stove. He was a gentleman and made me laugh a lot. I loved being with him and truly cared about him. After enjoying his friendship for two years, I provoked an advance on his part. He later confided how afraid he had been of making the wrong move and ruining his chances with me. He moved in with me a year later.

Pierre and I had to travel to my hometown. He decided it was too far to drive, so we took a plane instead. Because I was scared of heights, Pierre took the time to convince me that I had no reason to be afraid of flying in the eight-passenger plane.

But when we arrived at the airport, I panicked. "You told me it was a big plane. I'm not flying in that toy."

Pierre put his arm around my shoulders as we walked toward the plane. "Don't worry. Everything's going to be fine."

I had just put a foot on the first step when the wind caught under the wing and the plane started to move. "Are you crazy?" I shouted at Pierre. "The pilot can't even wait for us to be seated. I don't want to get in." I turned around and began to walk away but Pierre guided me back.

The next thing I knew, I was inside the plane. When I noticed there were only two other passengers, fear took over and I didn't think before talking. "If you think I'm flying in this thing, you're mistaken."

A young boy who was sitting next to his father looked up at me and said, "Ma'am, don't be afraid. It's all in your head."

I looked at him as if to say, "What do you know?" Yet I sat down, thinking that the child might have more sense than I did.

The plane took off. I didn't think I could hold my breath for so long. I exhaled for the first time once we were in the air. For the next hour, Pierre tried in vain to have me look out the window to admire the lakes. I refused. Instead, I gripped his trousers near the thigh and tightened my hold on him every time the plane encountered the least turbulence. I later noticed a huge bruise on Pierre's thigh and was surprised that he hadn't mentioned how tightly I had grasped his leg.

Six months later, on the first day of June, Pierre and I decided to get married. I invited Nanette and her husband for breakfast and didn't tell them about our marriage plans. Only my children knew and they were as happy as I was. We rode up the elevator to the highest floor in a downtown building.

Nanette noticed that there were no restaurants on the floor. "What's going on?"

I couldn't contain my excitement any longer. "This is City Hall. Pierre and I are getting married." After a brief ceremony, we all enjoyed brunch at a nearby restaurant.

That same afternoon, I was working in the garage when a neighbor passed by and asked me how I was. I answered that I was fine and that Pierre and I had got married that morning. Then I turned around and continued to work on the milling machine.

Six months later, Pierre arrived home with plane tickets to the Dominican Republic. We were leaving the next morning. He knew better than to give me too much time to panic.

I was thrilled as we headed toward the plane. Once on board, I looked at the people sitting on benches. Some passengers were holding onto ceiling straps and others were sitting back-to-back. I was terrified. "If you think your going to get me to fly thousands of miles in this thing, you're mistaken," I told Pierre.

Pierre gaped at me in surprise but said nothing. Everyone else stared at me.

I told an elderly man that my husband was insane, that he had once persuaded me to fly in a toy plane, and that he had no respect for me. I even yelled out that I wanted a divorce.

Pierre put his arms around me, told me not to worry, and showed me where the pilot sat.

I stared at the floor transmission, at the gas gauge, and the miles per hour gauge. I had a panic attack and frantically tried to get off the plane. "You're crazy if you think I'm flying in this thing. There's only one clock." My legs went weak when I saw the gas and brake pedal. I wanted out, I wanted a divorce, and I never wanted to see Pierre again. I calmed down only after I understood that I wasn't in a plane but in a shuttle bus that was transporting us to the plane.

"I'm sorry, honey, I couldn't believe you thought this was the plane," Pierre said, laughing.

I didn't feel very comfortable sitting in the plane, but I decided to calm down since I was certain other passengers were whispering about me. At one point, the stewardess distributed some candies. Just as I put one in my mouth, the plane hit an air pocket and I inhaled the candy. I was choking but managed to get out of my seat and into the aisle. Pierre was busy watching a movie and didn't notice what was happening to me.

All of a sudden, I felt strong arms grab me from behind. The candy popped out of my mouth and fell to the floor. Only then did Pierre look up at me and ask me what was going on.

Pierre and I had no idea on what the future held for us, but we were certain we had done the right thing by getting married. Unfortunately, I put him through hell during the first five years. Nightmares returned and triggered familiar feelings of fear, distrust, and unworthiness. My heart was on high alert again, and I fought the inner battle with a fierce determination. I promised myself that Pierre wouldn't hurt me, that I'd be the one to hurt him first. I had a plan. I wouldn't fall in love to the point where I'd lose my independence and self-control.

At first, I was unaware that the dormant pain inside me activated arguments between us—a pain that clung to my sentences as I raged out at Pierre. I couldn't explain why my words were so hurtful. "It's not what I meant to say" became my most common excuse.

But Pierre had the ability to decode my words before acting on them. He stood his ground and never wavered. He was a joker and kept me laughing. He played music, sang, and filled my life with joy. We exchanged inner gifts. He taught me how to laugh at myself and I taught him patience.

Even after I inflicted exhaustive bouts of mental torture on Pierre, he was still there, telling me that he loved me and that he understood where I was coming from. It was over. My anger and insecurities had vanished. I accepted the fact that he wouldn't hurt me, even when I'd push him to the limits of his endurance. Only when I finally believed I was safe did I begin to trade specks of uncertainty for trust.

We both won the great battle in the long run. Had it not been for Pierre's relentless faith and love, I would most likely have been alone again, making friends with the wind until my last breath.

Chapter 45
Stay With Me

Mom grew quite ill and lonely, so I offered to move her from the old age home and bring her home to live with us. Her room was upstairs, next to mine. I decorated it with white lace curtains and a white chenille bedspread, a small dresser, and a comfortable chair. Mom's colorful pillows on the bed and personal pictures on the walls, along with the scent of her perfume, gave the room a warm inviting ambiance.

Mom and I would sit on her bed for hours and reminisce, opening our hearts to each other. She confided in me and told me stories of her youth I had never heard before. Whenever she'd wonder why her life with Hugh had been so short, I tried to explain it in positive terms. "You had four wonderful years with him, Mom. You should be thankful."

"I know, I know, but I miss him and I wish I could tell him that," she said, her eyes filling with tears.

"What's stopping you, Mom? Do it. It'll help," I said.

"I know. I just wish...." Mom stopped talking and bowed her head. I knew what she meant. I had also once said, "I wish."

One evening I walked into Mom's bedroom with her favorite—a bottle of brandy. "Mom, I need to talk to you and I want you to listen." I sat on the bed and poured her a glass of brandy. "I know that what I'm about to say will hurt you. I'm sorry, but I must get rid of baggage that's too heavy for me."

Mom lay back on her pillow, a puzzled look on her face. "What is it? What's bothering you?"

I began to relate the problems I had had with her father, then I moved on to the priest, my wedding, my first baby, then Dad and all the other things Mom had pretended not to have noticed or known about. Nothing was going to stop me. I needed to discuss issues from the past that still tormented me and I was convinced that she did too.

Mom sipped glass after glass of brandy and came up with excuses for every question I put forward. Then she began to cry. She remained secretive about her father and refused to elaborate on any topic that concerned him. Not even brandy would reveal those deep and painful memories.

I held her in my arms and we cried together. "Mom, I'm not sorry that we had this conversation; it was long overdue."

She held onto my hand. With teary eyes, she said, "I've never been happier since I've been living here with you."

We had dealt with a load of questions and had been compensated with relief and understanding. "Mom, thanks for listening. Our talk helped me to shed a big burden." I felt good and I believed she did too.

"I always thought you were the strong one and that it wasn't necessary to explain or dwell on things. I realize now how wrong I was," Mom said before she fell asleep.

Mom was seventy-nine and weighed seventy-five pounds. We agreed that when caring for her became overwhelming for me or when she felt it was time to obtain specialized care elsewhere, we'd be honest with each other. I came home from work one day and noticed that Mom had packed a few of her belongings. "It's time for me to go," she said, a sad look on her face.

"Oh, Mom, are you sure?"

"It's time. They have my room ready."

The day she was placed in the palliative care institute, she weighed less than fifty pounds and her health was deteriorating at a rapid pace. Daily visits became part of my schedule. I prepared meals that had to be processed through a blender, and then fed them to her with a syringe. I made arrangements with the owner of a spa to have Mom go there two or three times a week at five in the morning before any other customers arrived. I'd take Mom to the spa where she enjoyed the hot tub and pool for an hour while I kept her afloat in the water.

"This has got to be the closest thing to heaven," Mom would say, over and over.

Mom had lost all muscle mass and her skin hung from her bones. The doctors and staff were amazed at her reluctance to let go.

#

Nanette was adopted and Mom felt it wasn't necessary to tell her who her biological parents were. When we questioned her about Nanette, Mom would hyperventilate and check her heartbeat right away, making it impossible for us to insist on an explanation.

Whispers had caught my attention at a young age. Aunts and uncles and cousins seemed to know more about Nanette than we did. Nanette would worry and get frustrated because she knew they were whispering about her.

"It won't make any difference to me, Mom. She's my sister. Please tell me," I'd plead with her.

Mom waited until the last moment of her life to whisper something in Nanette's ear. As hard as Nanette strained to understand what Mom was trying to tell her, she couldn't. Maybe it was a revelation about her birth parents, but we'll never know. I felt bad that Nanette never discovered the truth. Mom was selfish in keeping this secret to herself.

Mom was buried next to her first love. She made me promise to bury her in a dress she had bought at a garage sale. She liked it because it hid the neck bones and her tiny arms. Even months after her death, I had a hard time accepting the fact she was gone. I'd walk up the stairs of the old age home where Mom had stayed, only to snap out of my daze and head back home.

Chapter 46
Feelings

At two in the morning, I awoke with an ominous feeling that chilled me to the bones. An unfamiliar pain deep inside me made breathing difficult. I was afraid and couldn't understand why such a cold sweat had come over me all of a sudden. It wasn't menopause—those symptoms had stopped long ago. I decided to go downstairs and make a hot chocolate.

As I entered the kitchen, a white shadow passed beside me and headed toward the living room. I thought that Pierre had followed me downstairs, but I could still hear his snores coming from the bedroom. I assumed he was playing a trick on me and I turned around. "Who is that? Is that you, Pierre?"

When I heard more snores coming from the bedroom, I was certain it wasn't him. I was just about to heat up some milk when I felt a shiver go down my spine and a sharp pain in my chest. I thought I was having a heart attack. "I'd better go back to bed," I whispered out loud.

I ran up the stairs and jumped into bed close to Pierre. I was cold, in pain, and scared, but I eventually fell asleep.

Later that morning, the phone rang. "Are you Daniel's mother?" a man at the other end of the line asked me.

"Yes, I am." I figured that maybe Daniel had done something silly again.

"I'm a police officer. I'm calling to tell you that your son is dead. He committed suicide."

My stomach felt queasy and my blood turned cold. The same deep pain carved itself into my chest. Everything went black for a moment. "Oh, he's in the hospital. All right, I'll go and see him." I hung up.

I don't remember anything after that. I went about my chores as if nothing had happened. The children came to the house, and I couldn't understand why they had all come to visit at the same time. They seemed saddened about something, but I still puttered along as if nothing were wrong.

Someone called an ambulance to bring me to the hospital. When the doctor asked me what was wrong, I replied, "I watched a terrible movie and threw it away."

"Where is it?" he asked.

"It's in your trash can. I don't recommend it."

A few days later, Pierre brought me to the family doctor. I told him about the movie. I was asked about my children and my reply was that nothing eventful was going on. There was talk of putting me in the hospital if my memory didn't return.

I didn't recall going to the funeral or seeing Daniel in the coffin. Someone told me that I thought Daniel was Sam but that I couldn't understand why the children were all grown up. In a matter of seconds, I had regressed twenty-five years in memory.

#

Though I believe Daniel's death is recent, eight years have already passed. I've blocked out my son's passing for fear that it might break my heart. But the pain must be released. Year after year, my mind and body lose their grip on sanity because I know Daniel is gone and I can't face the truth.

I'm sitting in a psychologist's office asking for help—help in triggering my memory past the phone call that announced Daniel had committed suicide. I focus on the psychologist. She is a beautiful woman. Her eyes and voice show compassion and understanding. I know I can speak to her. I begin by saying anything that goes through my mind. Ironically, I try to avoid the subject I came here to discuss in the first place. We laugh and I continue to talk about myself to break the ice.

Sooner or later, the conversation shifts to my son and me, and to others who were affected by his passing. My time is soon up. I'll come back in a week. But the psychologist asks me to do something before then. She asks me to write a letter to Daniel. I experience unfamiliar feelings—extreme anxiety and dizziness that I can't control—so I dismiss the idea of writing a letter as a waste of time.

I find myself sitting at the computer on the evening before my next appointment. I'm aware of two words: *Hi Daniel*. My hands hold the key to my emotions as they fly over the keyboard, but I'm unaware of what I'm writing. The flow of tears is so intense that I can't see the words on the screen.

It's over. I can't say anything more. I feel relief, though my eyes feel heavy. I look in the mirror and see bags of tears that have not yet found their way out. They're waiting for emotions to trigger a flow that is long overdue.

I'm back in the psychologist's office. I begin a conversation with her, but I'm distracted. I know that she'll ask me for the letter I stashed away in my purse. She smiles. I hear what she's asking. I feel my chest cave in as I hand her the letter. She smiles again as she reads it, nods her head as if she agrees with what I've written.

I sit impatiently, wondering if she can read between the lines. Will she understand my reluctance in letting Daniel go? I must face the truth. My body and mind show signs of hidden pain that will destroy me in due course. I can't cling to lies, even though they've become my beliefs. I must set Daniel free. At the same time, I will be free.

Prayers are frequent. I say a certain prayer every day since the birth of my first son, Matthew. I ask God to spare me from ever having to be one of the unfortunate people who experience the death of a child. This prayer is a belief that exists only in my mind, a lie hidden for so long that it serves as a crutch for survival. I must let go of this crutch; otherwise, the rest of my life will be useless.

Hi Daniel,

I miss you. I wish you were here in person and not just in my mind and heart. I need to hug you until my arms lose their strength. I need to feel you and hear your voice. I have lost track of time; my life is on hold as I weep and wait for you. I know this is impossible, but at times I feel as if you're here. I'm having a terrible time letting you go.

I should be thankful to have had you for thirty-three years. I was blessed to have been your mother. My mind wanders to the day you were born. My memories of your life are still so vivid that the sound of your voice and the scent of your aftershave keep me confined to a circle that has no exit.

Please help me to let go because I can't succeed on my own. You are strong and I need you to release the grip I have on you. I need to breathe on my own.

Our lives together were full of joy and happiness but overwhelmed with sadness that neither one of us understood. Your pain was deep and your final decision was to end your life, but it affected the lives of so many others who loved you.

You've accomplished what you lived for and your leaving was premature, but I understand. Your pain was so intense that you chose to put an end to it. It put an end to my life as it was. Now I'm in limbo, hanging on to emptiness, and the grip is so strong. You're the only one who has the power to release me.

Daniel, I love you so much. The love in my heart can't be replaced for it belongs to you. I know that you're free of the earthly burdens you had to endure and I also know that you're happy. In my mind, I see your smile and the pure glow in your eyes—just like you had when you were a child. But you need me to let go and I feel that now I might just try to do so. Please let me continue to feel your presence, even if it's only in my mind, for soon we must part and it'll be the hardest thing I've ever had to do. Daniel, please forgive me for anything I did that might have added to your pain. Forgiveness is necessary if we want to heal.

Please God, be a guide for his beautiful sons. May they be released of any inner pain so they can see clearly their reason for living. I love them and will always be here for them.

I have so much to say but my mind is overwhelmed. I love you, Daniel, and want you to experience all the joys and happiness you were deprived of here on earth, for it was only a temporary visit.

All my love and hugs. I can't say goodbye. Please help me. This is the hardest thing I've ever had to do. I love you.

I leave the psychologist's office feeling somewhat relieved. I realize that I'm on the way to accepting my loss. I need to admit this fact because my heart has been on hold long enough. I'll see the psychologist again in a week and I must write another letter, but at the moment, I can't find the words because they're jumbled like loose pieces of a scrabble game.

I meet with the psychologist the following week. We chat for a few moments and I hand her my letter.

Hi Daniel,

I think of you all the time. Christmas is just around the corner. I remember how the whole family had gathered together last Christmas to celebrate. Now that you're gone, it's not the same. The others have distanced themselves and celebrations are rare.

Daniel, do you remember how you always happened to be where the action was? If anything special happened in town, you were there. Well, something exciting is happening right now. Right here in my heart. I'm going to try to set you free. By doing this, I'll release the pain that has haunted me.

I understand that it's very selfish of me to hang on to you like this. I'm probably inflicting pain on you and it becomes a never-ending circle.

Daniel, I'm inviting you into my heart one more time, just so that I can say goodbye. I suppose you've already done this and I thank you for coming to see me before you left. When I woke up that night, when my body was chilled to the core and I stood breathless in the kitchen, I knew something bad had happened. But I would never have imagined it had happened to you.

You gave me a gift by showing up that night. I knew it wasn't a dream when I saw a shadow drift down the hallway. Nothing could have chilled me to such an extent that blankets provided little warmth. While I focused on my pain, you were considerate and loving and took a moment to walk through my home one last time. It was your way of saying goodbye and I thank you for showing me that you cared enough to do so.

The most important thing is that you are free. Just know that my love for you grows stronger every day and I will pray for you.

Thank you, Daniel, for choosing me to be your mother. It was a privilege. I love you.

I sit at my computer, close my eyes, and write you another letter. The words make their way from my heart through dense emotions. I stop when the pain becomes unbearable.

Hi Daniel,

Good and bad memories fly through my mind.

I remember how active you were as a child and how I couldn't cope because you were always one step ahead of me. I should have taken the time to understand why your actions were so self-destructive, but I didn't, couldn't, or wouldn't—or maybe all of the above.

When you were a mischievous young boy, I found that brushing off the troublesome incidents and blaming you was easier than looking for the truth. I was young and inexperienced, but it was no excuse. I could see how fast you were racing toward a sad ending to your life. I didn't know what to do or how to reach you, except to comfort you during the times you confided in me. I wanted you to understand that you weren't inferior to your brothers, as you believed you were, and that you had talent you weren't aware of.

The Bible preaches to reach out to the hurting lamb, the one most in need. I failed to do so because I believed the task was impossible. Maybe I should have tried harder and not given up as easily as I did. You heard my warnings, but maybe they should have been louder. I think I was clinging to my own sanity. Forgive me, Daniel. I'm sorry I was so weak. The warnings were painful and my attempts to help you were in vain.

I know you tried several times without success to get off the fast track, but the temptation was too powerful. I remember how you predicted your early death.

I'm grateful that almost all our conversations ended with "I love you." These words echo in my mind every day. You'll remain in my heart because the joys of having loved you and the pain of having lost you have left their scars forever. I love you so much.

Mom XX

I visit the psychologist and bring my letters. Sometimes I feel as if I'm taking a step backward. It's a constant fight to hold on to my sanity. Letter after letter, the pain still tightens its grip on my heart.

Hi Daniel,

Again, I wish you were here. Again, I go against reality and wash away any progress in the works.

I keep remembering when you were young and how I didn't spend enough time with you. Wasted time was plentiful. I try to understand, but I end up at the same place: the beginning.

I'm angry that you ran away. I'm angry that I couldn't stop you. I'm angry because a part of my heart has died and I can't feel anything the way I did before.

My love for you is mixed with so many emotions. It lingers, then fades away, only to bring me back to wishing you were here. Every time I try to accept the fact that you're gone, my heart stands in the way and sheds tears that flood any logical path I was about to take.

I hope that, one day, my heart will beat to a normal rhythm without skipping because you are the fifth of six beats that complete the cycle of my life.

Hi Daniel,

I went to the graveyard to see you, but you weren't there. I grew tired of waiting for you to come to me. I wondered why your name wasn't on the tombstone next to your father's. I thought I had seen it, but maybe it was my imagination. I get confused at times.

I feel that you're near, but I can't see you. The scent of your aftershave fills the air every so often and makes me feel lightheaded. I know you're here, but I can't touch you. I'm angry at the thought that you're behind an invisible wall.

I'm tired of waiting. I want to hold you. I want to hug you. I want you to know how much I love you.

Please help me get out of this circle that has no exit.

Bye, Daniel.

This last visit stood out from the others. When I left the psychologist's office, a faint aroma of aftershave breezed by me and I felt a hand squeeze mine. I walked through the waiting room, wondering why people were smiling at me, until I realized that I was the one smiling. I continued my walk down the hall and still felt the firm grip on my hand. When I approached the exit and opened the door, the grasp on my hand slipped away.

I was alone again, but it was different. What on earth had just happened? But I already knew the answer. My heart skipped a beat as I drove home. I had a secret. We had a secret.

#

I later discovered that Daniel had been born with an emotional deficiency that had caused turmoil in his life. It saddens me that help wasn't available for him then, which leads me to believe that we are sometimes our own worst enemy. After many visits to the psychologist and many letters to Daniel, I still couldn't remember his death and funeral. However, I did learn to accept it and was given a gift much more meaningful: more time with Daniel.

One cold winter night, I went downstairs to get a glass of water in the kitchen. I couldn't help but notice something glowing outside. My curiosity was aroused and I peeked through the blinds. I saw a ray of light shining over a bench placed under the kitchen window. A little boy was sitting on the bench.

I opened the back door. Light shone around the little boy. Barefoot and in my pajamas, I went outside, sat next to him, and put his hand in mine. I could see the snow a few feet ahead, but I felt warm where we were sitting. I glanced at the boy and was surprised to see that it was Daniel. He was three years old and I was in my twenties. I held his hand tightly in case he'd let go. There was no notion of time as we sat hand in hand without saying a word. All the while, rain, windstorms, hail, sun, snow, ice, tornadoes, and terrifying black clouds rolled across the sky in all their fury.

The storms passed and the sky was calm again. Daniel's hand wasn't as tiny anymore and the arthritis in my body was unmistakably there. I looked at him. He was thirty-three and I was older. I closed my eyes and turned away, then felt his hand slip out of mine. When I opened my eyes, a monarch butterfly fluttered its wings and flew off.

I woke up. My hand was warm and clenched tight, and my heart was beating fast. I was overcome with emotion, but I wasn't afraid. I was finally at peace because I had learned the truth.

I visited the psychologist the next day and we agreed that I didn't need to see her anymore. After we exchanged warm hugs and said goodbye, I left with a feeling of acceptance. In my dream, Daniel and I had spent precious time together, revisiting the good and bad periods of his short life. I had experienced a more powerful meaning of love. With the exception of my love for God, no unconditional love was stronger than the love I had for my child.

Chapter 47
Shared Pain

I'd try to go back home each year to visit my brother Timmy. He had bought a house and had had a few girlfriends but had later chosen to live his life as a bachelor.

As I drove up Main Street, I remembered my life and how difficult it had been to escape the grip that this small town had had on me. But I did have some good memories, especially about Andy. He had been a special friend to me and had taught me about laughter, dancing, tenderness, self-esteem, and how good it felt to fall in love—butterflies and all. I had heard that Andy had lost his only son to suicide a year after Daniel had committed suicide, so I decided to call him and see how he was doing.

Andy picked up the phone at the other end of the line. How could I ever forget that voice? He seemed surprised yet happy to hear from me. We agreed to meet for coffee.

My stomach was in knots while I waited for Andy near the lobby payphone. One of my girlfriends had accompanied me on the trip to town. Since I was married, I felt it was more appropriate that she join Andy and me for coffee.

A car drove up and Andy stepped out. As we hugged, that same special feeling ran through me. It wasn't sexual but rather an emotion that implied sincere affection. The last time I saw Andy, I was thirty-eight years old. I couldn't believe we were face to face again after twenty-five years. We had changed. He was thinner and I had gained weight, but when I looked into his eyes, I saw sadness shadowing happiness.

We sat in a restaurant and reminisced about our children.

Andy explained the tragedy of having lost a son who had played a large part in his life. I felt terrible for Andy and could relate to his pain. His son had written a letter in which he explained that his suicide was a decision he had willingly made. Andy was to call his son's closest friends, take the savings his son had accumulated and, on the Thursday after the funeral, celebrate with them.

While Andy was bringing us up to date with details about his life, my heart was breaking. He was diabetic, had had his thyroid gland removed, and had suffered a heart attack a few years earlier. Although he had mellowed somewhat and showed signs of physical and mental pain, the tender gaze in his eyes remained the same. He was still the beautiful man I had known so many years earlier.

What surprised me the most was that Andy and his wife had separated months after I had left town. As the evening ended and we said our goodbyes, the song, "You don't know me," by Ray Charles played in the background of my mind.

I was extremely happy to arrive home the next day. I hugged Pierre, grateful that I had found the right person for me.

Chapter 48
Sweet Memories

I've experienced more sweet memories than I could have ever expected. They're stored in my heart where they're protected from intrusion. Monarch butterflies trigger memories of the wonderful people I cared about who had short but meaningful lives. Though life is painful at times, I realize that it is a gift, and I'm grateful to have received so much love from so many people.

The tears I sometimes cry today are the ones whose natural flow was suppressed by fear or pride long ago. Even so, unpleasant incidents from the past don't seem as awful anymore because they're out in the open, instead of festering inside me. If there are any empty spaces in my memory bank, it's because I store only the important remembrances and take the time to enjoy them.

#

Every one of my children and grandchildren is unique, and each one has the power to touch my heart. I feel for them, fear for them, and love them unconditionally. They are wonderful young people whose spirits are filled with adventure, ready to take on the future. I accumulate memories of their hugs, their smiles, and their innocent expressions—untarnished images that I've been privileged to see. I'm saddened at the thought that Sam didn't live to enjoy the gentle hug of his grandchild and the irresistible power of love that flows from a young heart.

My mind drifts off now and then and I find myself laughing out loud. I laugh at the memory of a desperate morning phone call from my eight-year-old grandson Félix and a friend who had celebrated a birthday the night before. I laugh about how I jumped in the truck and rushed over with a large bottle of Pepto-Bismol, the magic cure, to find the two boys dancing the Pepto-Bismol dance on the veranda. Their faces were drained from a sleepless night, but they still managed to smile when they saw me drive up. Oh, sweet memories!

The feeling of a child's hug as they latch onto me is precious. For an instant, I experience true innocent love. I don't want to let go but I must. I'm blessed with many young grandchildren who often express their love for me, so hugs and kisses are plentiful. I'll leave this world, never to have refused the gift of a hug.

I have experienced robotic hugs when you feel you must hug but don't really want to.

Surprise hugs, where the person you decided to hug is too surprised to react.

Hypocritical hugs, where it seemed to be the right thing to do at the moment.

Comforting hugs, which are always appreciated.

Sexual hugs, where unexpected feelings surface.

Unattainable hugs, where the "hugee" has no idea what to do and his arms hang by his side.

Pure and genuine hugs of a child.

Hugs that draw you inside the other and cause you to forget your surroundings.

All these hugs are priceless when the intention is sincere. The exception is the hug of deceit, where sin motivates the selfish acts of the person who preys upon the innocent.

#

As I question whether it's a myth or a fact that souls choose their lives beforehand, I'm aware that I willingly accepted the challenge I inherited, for it was one that I met with energy and inner satisfaction. I admit that life's lessons were presented to me in somewhat of a condensed manner since I learned them through hardship upon hardship. But they served their purpose: they taught me the true value of life.

Many experiences challenged me to the limits of my abilities, but I was rewarded with love and respect that my soul wears with pride. I have no regrets, since every moment was a step toward my life's goal. I travel lightly now. Like anyone with credentials after their name, I too have a prestigious title attached to mine: L.I.V.E.D.

I think of earlier days and of promises of blue and pink dresses. Certain memories bring a smile to my face, but tears flow once in a while because I can still see the pain that my children have stored in the back of their minds. The concept that we as parents were their most important role models seemed to have slipped through the cracks when they needed it the most.

I sit across a table from my children and sometimes visualize them as the little tots they once were. Events of their early years play over and over in my mind like slides in an old movie projector. Although tangible pictures are few, my mind holds a lifetime of images: one of every smile, every tear, every hug, and every occasion that caused my heart to sing.

My thoughts and life are dedicated to my children. My heart overflows with love for them; however, there's a place in it for anyone who has blessed my life. If I could bottle all my wasted time and reuse it, it would certainly be with my children. Everything I've wished I could do but didn't, or couldn't, I've done in my dreams.

My children call me almost daily. "Just wanted to know how you were, Mom," they begin the conversation. I look forward to the ringing of the phone, anticipating whom I'll be privileged to speak to next.

#

Charlie, now a grown man with fine-looking children of his own, was sitting at the kitchen table across from me. We were chatting and playing a game of Cribbage when he took my hands in his
and said, "How are you, Mom?"

"I'm fine," I replied.

"No, how are you really?"

When he asked me the second time, we were looking straight into each other's eyes and holding hands. For a fraction of a second, I felt as if Charlie and I were one. An intense shock ran along my spine. We sat looking at each other, speechless, and then Charlie let go of my hands.

The next day, Charlie called. "Mom?"

"What is it?" I asked.

"Nothing, Mom. It's okay."

He called back the next day but was unable to tell me what was on his mind. On the third day, he confided in me. "When we were sitting at the table the other day, the strangest feeling came over me. I felt as if we were one, and then I felt an intense shock all along my spine."

I was stunned. How could he have felt the same thing I did?

"What do you think it meant?" Charlie asked.

I didn't understand it myself, but I answered, "I think it was to show you how much I love you, Charlie."

We left it at that, but the memory of that wonderful moment often crosses my mind.

On another occasion, Charlie and I were reminiscing about the past. "Mom, I remember Granddad's blue eyes and the unmistakable mean look he projected. I'd deliberately give away my points in Cribbage because I was afraid to win," Charlie said. "I'll never forget his face."

#

The innocence of my youth was short-lived. As a defenseless child, I was often at the mercy of vultures that waited for a weak moment before leaving their lasting stain on me. They stole my freedom and a clear vision of my life with all its hopes and dreams.

As I began to understand why each day had been such an uphill battle, I gradually gained the ability and courage to sort through the excess baggage in my mind and identify what truly belonged to me. I determined that the dosage of insecurity, guilt, hatred, and mistrust injected in my ancestors during their innocent youth was much more powerful than the dosage they had injected into me. Unaware of it at the time, I had replicated these feelings for my children's innocent minds to absorb.

It took me a lifetime to sort through the personal baggage imposed on me at a young age—baggage that hindered my every thought and destroyed the slightest dream I attempted to cultivate. Then again, if I had had the opportunity to get rid of excess baggage earlier in my life, I might have been deprived of the special gift of forgiveness.

Looking back, I understand how religion and its authorities molded me into a puppet and slave, and overwhelmed me with guilt for having defied their *Thou Shalt Not* teachings. Now I can suppress those branded beliefs whenever they try to surface and claim their importance in my existence.

I'm grateful for having experienced love and pain to its extreme and for having reaped life's rewards. Faith, hope, and forgiveness were essential to my survival, but the most difficult part was tapping into my strength and capability.

As my self-esteem grew, mirrors began to reflect my true image. Harsh words were not kept as dead weight. The spiritual vision of my meaning on earth became clearer. I emptied the drawers of my mind of stagnant negativity, lingering revenge, and unhealed pain. I destroyed the roots to wipe out any chance of regrowth. I visualized the discarded contents as black pieces of lint slipping away and disintegrating into thin air. Although the road to happiness was an agonizing process, I've cleansed myself of guilt and regrets that didn't belong to me.

Now my mind holds joyful memories. Sorrow and pain also hold their place, making my emotions sincere. Every day is sprinkled with love and satisfaction. Trivial things aren't important. I concentrate on inner beauty and see it in everyone I meet.

My life with Pierre ends with an "I love you" every night. I'm a penniless millionaire and I want for nothing. I find pleasure in simple things, like a sunset that reflects the golden glitter off the water, or a breeze that fills my lungs with the smell of blossoms and fresh air. Hummingbirds and butterflies, flowers and fruit trees are plentiful. The sound of a flickering fireplace comforts me. The front door is unlocked for there is no fear. My welcome mat supports a never-ending list of guests and the sound of children's laughter often fills the air. My home is serene and cozy and decorated with love.

In the meantime, I sit with Pierre and wonder, "Where have the last twenty-four years gone?"

Life is beautiful. I knew I'd eventually find happiness and, being the adventurous person I was, I took the long road to heaven.

I love you.

The End

www.ingramcontent.com/pod-product-compliance
Ingram Content Group UK Ltd.
Pitfield, Milton Keynes, MK11 3LW, UK
UKHW040602210726
13854UKWH00008B/1841